M000208966

A Guide to U.S. Environmental Law

A Guide to U.S.
Environmental Law

ARDEN ROWELL AND JOSEPHINE VAN ZEBEN

UNIVERSITY OF CALIFORNIA PRESS

University of California Press
Oakland, California

© 2021 by Arden Rowell and Josephine van Zeben

Library of Congress Cataloging-in-Publication Data

Names: Rowell, Arden, author. | Zeben, Josephine A. W.
    van, 1984– author.
Title: A guide to U.S. environmental law / Arden Rowell
    and Josephine van Zeben.
Other titles: Guide to US environmental law
Description: Oakland, California : University of
    California Press, [2021] | Includes bibliographical
    references and index.
Identifiers: LCCN 2020037013 (print) | LCCN 2020037014
    (ebook) | ISBN 9780520295230 (hardcover) |
    ISBN 9780520295247 (paperback) |
    ISBN 9780520968066 (ebook)
Subjects: LCSH: Environmental law—United States. |
    Environmental impact charges—Law and
    legislation—United States.
Classification: LCC KF3817 .R69 2021 (print) | LCC KF3817
    (ebook) | DDC 344.7304/6—dc23
LC record available at https://lccn.loc.gov/2020037013
LC ebook record available at https://lccn.loc.
gov/2020037014

Manufactured in the United States of America

29 28 27 26 25 24 23 22 21
10 9 8 7 6 5 4 3 2 1

For our families—past, present, and future

Contents

Illustrations

FIGURES

TABLES

Spotlight Boxes

Preface

How should humans shape the world in which they live? Countries around the world have crafted different answers to this question. This volume summarizes the way that the United States has answered it through the vehicle of environmental law.

Most resources on environmental law are written for lawyers who are already well versed in the legal system of a particular country. While those resources are valuable for specialists, we believe they have two important limitations.

First, by limiting their audience to law students or lawyers, traditional environmental law resources exclude many stakeholders of environmental law. Environmental problems affect everyone, and scientists and social scientists, policymakers and activists, citizens and students, all have important roles to play in how the environment is governed and protected. One fundamental purpose of this book is to reach these audiences by explaining the environmental law of the United States without assuming that the reader has any prior legal training in U.S. law.

Second, because environmental problems—such as pollution, ecosystem degradation, and climate change—share many similarities regardless of where they are located, there is much to be learned from comparative approaches to environmental law. Yet traditional environmental law resources are optimized for domestic legal specialists, not comparative scholars. This book is different. Distinctively, it was written contemporaneously with its companion volume on the environmental law of the European Union (EU). Both volumes seek to distill the essential elements of environmental law, and both volumes follow the same modularized structure, which was designed to facilitate comparisons.

Both books begin with the building blocks of domestic environmental law: an overview of key legal actors, types of law, and regulatory tools that the United States (or the EU) uses to address environmental problems. The second part of each book delves into specific environmental issues that environmental law regulates: pollution, ecosystem management, and climate change. In future, this structure will be echoed in other books in this series, allowing for easy comparisons between how the United States deals with environmental problems through law, and how other jurisdictions tackle the same issues.

We believe this book provides a long-overdue resource on environmental law for those who work in environmental policy or environmental science. It can also act as a brief textbook for an undergraduate or foreign course on environmental law, and as a starting point for comparative environmental scholars. Readers intent on in-depth study of particular environmental laws will find the book helpful for orientation and context, and will find suggestions for more traditional specialized resources at the end of the book.

Environmental law is a diverse, complex, and ever-changing area of law that addresses some of society's biggest challenges. By boiling down the essentials of environmental law, we hope to encourage meaningful dialogue across disciplinary and national borders, between environmental lawyers and other environmental practitioners, and among environmental lawyers in different jurisdictions. Humans necessarily affect the environments in which they live. By sharing ideas and improving the understanding of how laws around the world shape the environment, we hope to help in identifying strategies for increasing environmental quality and, in turn, for promoting human flourishing.

PART ONE

Building Blocks of U.S. Environmental Law

CHAPTER ONE

Regulating Environmental Impacts

Environmental law regulates human behavior in light of its environmental impacts. Environmental impacts affect the surroundings or conditions in which humans, plants, and animals function. Every country around the world has developed its own legal (and nonlegal) approaches to addressing environmental impacts. These responses are based in part on normative choices about what a good environment would look like, and are informed by historical, natural, cultural, and political conditions that tend to vary widely within and between countries.

To understand how the United States—or any country—approaches environmental law, it is important to understand the distinctive challenges that are presented by regulating the environment. Environmental impacts affect the environment in which people live, rather than affecting people directly. While humans can change their environments—by taking actions that affect environmental quality, such as littering or picking up litter, emitting or reducing air pollutants, cutting down or planting trees—any effect of those actions on human well-being will be indirect, as a result of subsequent human exposure to the degraded or improved environment. Some environmental impacts may have very few important implications for humans, while others may have profound implications for human health, well-being, and flourishing. Understanding the implications of human actions for environmental quality, and the implications of environmental quality for human ends, thus presents special challenges to environmental regulation.

This chapter begins by introducing the core challenges to environmental law that are created by the fundamental characteristics of environmental impacts: namely, that those impacts tend to be diffuse through space and time, complex, and nonhuman in character. It then flags key normative values and choices that the United States has made regarding environmental impacts, which undergird the U.S. approach to environmental law. Understanding these background normative choices can help readers in approaching the remainder of the book, which further develops the key actors, types of law, and specific strategies the United States has deployed to address particular environmental problems.

KEY CHALLENGES IN REGULATING ENVIRONMENTAL IMPACTS

Many challenges in environmental regulation can be traced back to three characteristics of environmental impacts (table 1). First, because the environment is both durable and dynamic, many environmental impacts are diffuse through space and time. A person who tosses a plastic bottle on the ground does not merely affect that place in that moment; the bottle may be washed away to a distant spot, or even a distant ocean, and it may take hundreds of years to degrade into microplastics, which then may affect the environment for hundreds of years more. Few, if any, of these impacts may be apparent to the person who threw the bottle on the ground in the first place, and even experts may have a difficult time predicting exactly where and when the plastic will generate environmental impacts.

Second, the impacts of human action on the environment tend to be complex. Natural environmental systems are already complex before humans become involved; it should not be surprising that it is still more complicated to predict the full implications of human action on natural

TABLE I

Characteristics of Environmental Impacts

Characteristic	Impact	Regulatory Challenge
Diffusion	Environmental consequences are often *geographically and spatially distant* from the human activities that caused those consequences.	Detecting and predicting the environmental impacts of human (in)action
Complexity	Environmental consequences tend to be *obscure, technical, and interactive*. Many small individual actions may combine in complicated ways to create a single impact; a single action may have multiple impacts; and the type(s) of those impacts may be difficult to measure, understand, and/or solve.	Gathering and interpreting information about environmental impacts Tracing causal connections between human actions and consequences
Nonhuman	Environmental consequences tend to relate to the *nonhuman animals, plants, and processes* that make up much of human surroundings.	Identifying (or creating) a nexus between human behavior and the nonhuman environment Meaningfully representing nonhuman interests

environments, and to predict the follow-on effects of environmental quality on human well-being. Only in recent years have scientists started to understand the multiple implications of plastic waste, and of degraded microplastics, on natural environments and human health. Most likely, the extent of environmental and human impacts of plastic waste depends significantly on the scope and interaction of that waste—on how many people use and dispose of plastics, and in which ways, with what frequency, and in which locations. The environmental impacts of plastic disposal are therefore obscure, technical, and dependent upon knowledge—which will often be unavailable—about other human actions that may also affect the environment.

Third, consider that environmental impacts affect the natural environment, and that they therefore relate to the nonhuman animals, plants, and processes that make up much of human surroundings. Natural processes will eventually lead to the dispersion and decomposition of a plastic bottle that is thrown on the ground—but understanding and evaluating those natural processes presents challenges on its own. How will the plastic affect the particular ecosystem(s) into which it degrades? Which plants, animals, or fungi might be affected, how, and how acutely? Which other plants, animals, or fungi might be affected, in turn, by the direct impacts of environmental plastics on prey species or food sources? Which, if any, of these nonhuman effects impact human well-being? To what extent should nonhuman impacts matter for their own sake, even if they do not affect human well-being? Understanding the environmental impacts of human actions requires answering questions like these, and thus carries a special kind of informational, scientific, and normative burden.

Importantly, knowledge about an environmental impact does not guarantee legal action to remedy that impact. The environment cannot speak for itself; it depends on humans to do so on its behalf. The likelihood of a legal or social response differs depending on the perceived economic and social value of the environment to (a group of) individuals. This means that there are situations in which environmental impacts can go unnoticed, or unchecked, for long periods. At the same time, human law is able to directly regulate only human behavior. Environmental law must therefore identify a nexus between human behavior and the nonhuman environment, both to understand the impact of current human behaviors and to shape human behavior in directions that reflect a preferred relationship with the nonhuman environment.

THE ROLE OF NORMATIVE VALUES

Decisions about how to approach environmental problems are, explicitly or implicitly, decisions about how people want to shape the environment in which they live. This means that reasonable people might disagree as to whether U.S. strategies work well or poorly when measured against specific environmental problems. For example, the United States' decision to manage environmental impacts in large part through the vehicle of monetized cost-benefit analysis remains controversial even domestically. Moreover, it contrasts sharply with the approach of other jurisdictions—like the European Union—to the same problems. Similarly, the institutional choices jurisdictions make on how to address problems also embed normative choices. In the case of the United States, for instance, reliance on expert administrative agencies to set environmental policy tends to prioritize the value of scientific and technical expertise over the value of direct democratic accountability. As the book describes the distinctive characteristics of the U.S. approach to environmental problems, it is worth reflecting both on which normative choices underlie those approaches, and whether it would be possible to better them.

Another key normative question that is answered differently across jurisdictions relates to the management of environmental justice, which concerns the fairness of how environmental impacts are distributed (see spotlight 1). The challenge is ethical as well as practical: How should environmental harms and benefits ethically be spread across the (human and nonhuman) population? The U.S. legal system has no unified answer to the question of environmental justice, although its institutional and normative choices have implications for who bears environmental harms. For example, as we have already noted and as the next chapters explain further, U.S. environmental law relies heavily on cost-benefit analysis. Cost-benefit approaches typically address future impacts by monetizing environmental harms the same way regardless of when they accrue, and then discounting those monetized harms back to present value to account for the time-value of money. This has the normative implication that the U.S. government allocates fewer of today's dollars to prevent future harms than it allocates toward preventing immediate harms.

SPOTLIGHT 1. ENVIRONMENTAL JUSTICE

Environmental justice seeks to assure a fair distribution of environmental quality.

In the United States, locally undesirable land uses (LULUs)—such as landfills or incinerators—tend to be located near poor communities and communities of color. As a result, African American and Hispanic populations are disproportionately impacted by LULUs. Scholars disagree about whether existing distributions are the result of racist and/or classist siting decisions, market factors that constrain poor and nonwhite persons from moving away from LULUs, or both.

 U.S. environmental statutes typically do not address environmental justice concerns, though there are several presidential orders—most notably Executive Order 12,898—that encourage consideration of environmental justice and distributional implications. These are administered by the Office of Environmental Justice at the Environmental Protection Agency, which is the government body most closely affiliated with environmental justice goals.

SUMMARY

This chapter identified the distinguishing features of environmental impacts, and the challenges these impacts pose to crafting and implementing environmental law. It also flagged the importance of identifying the normative choices that are made in deciding on how to address environmental impacts through law.

TAKEAWAYS

✓ Using law to regulate environmental quality is challenging because environmental impacts tend to be diffuse through space and time, complex, and nonhuman in character.

✓ Different countries regulate environmental impacts differently. Many of the choices that countries make in regulating the environment reflect normative values.

KEY TERMS

AGENCIES Units of government created by statute.

COMPLEX IMPACTS Environmental impacts that are obscure, technical, and/or interactive. These can be difficult to measure, understand, and regulate.

COST-BENEFIT ANALYSIS A decision procedure for quantifying (and typically monetizing) the expected positive and negative impacts of a proposed policy.

DIFFUSE IMPACTS Environmental impacts that are geographically and/or spatially distant from the human actions that caused them.

DISCOUNTING The process of making future (monetary) amounts comparable to current amounts.

ENVIRONMENT The surroundings or conditions in which humans, plants, and animals function.

ENVIRONMENTAL IMPACTS Consequences (generally of human actions) for the surroundings or conditions in which humans, plants, and animals function.

ENVIRONMENTAL JUSTICE Fair distribution of environmental impacts.

ENVIRONMENTAL LAW The use of law to regulate human behaviors with environmental impacts.

NONHUMAN IMPACTS Environmental impacts that relate primarily or exclusively to nonhuman animals, plants, and processes.

REGULATIONS Binding rules of legal conduct issued by agencies; may also refer to the action or process, by any legal actor, of limiting or encouraging patterns of behavior.

DISCUSSION QUESTIONS

1. What are examples of diffuse environmental impacts? Which is harder to effectively address: impacts that are diffuse through space or impacts that are diffuse through time?

2. What should be the role of science and scientific information when considering environmental impacts? Can science alone solve complex problems?

3. How do nonhuman processes and humans interact to create environmental problems?

4. How should law address harms to the nonhuman environment?

5. What do you think is the most challenging feature of environmental impacts for the law: diffusion, complexity, or nonhuman character? Why?

6. What role should environmental justice play in environmental legal strategies?

CHAPTER TWO

Key Actors

This chapter introduces key actors in the U.S. legal landscape and describes how those actors work together (or not!) to create U.S. environmental law. Understanding who makes environmental law can be useful, since it indicates who has the power to make (or change) the law.

Three features of the U.S. government system are particularly critical for environmental law: the relationships between federal, state, and local governments; the separation of powers in the branches of the U.S. government; and the process of administrative regulation by administrative agencies.

FEDERAL, STATE, AND LOCAL ACTORS

In the United States, environmental law is largely driven by public actors—that is, members of the government.[1] The responsibilities and powers of government are fulfilled by three branches of government—the legislature, executive, and judiciary—each of which serves a different function.

In addition, in the United States, federal and state actors have a distinctive Constitutional status that defines much of their jurisdiction (that is, their power to make legally binding decisions) and can vary by subject matter and geographic location. This relationship is discussed in more detail below. The federal government plays a central (though not exclusive) role in regulating many environmental problems. That said, local governments also retain some important powers, particularly regarding local environmental issues. These powers are defined by state constitutions and therefore differ substantially among individual states and even among cities. In addition, Indian reservations—areas of land managed by indigenous Native American tribes—are controlled at least partially by tribal governments (see spotlight 2).[2]

The current allocation of authority between federal and state governments traces back to the founding of the United States and the ratification of the U.S. Constitution in 1789. The Constitution was drafted and ratified by representatives of thirteen former British colonies, which became the founding states of the United States. Over the subsequent two centuries, additional states joined, bringing the total number of U.S. states to fifty.[3] The authority of the federal government originates with the people of these individual states, which delegated some of their own power to the federal government upon forming or joining the union.

These historical developments mean that the scope of state and federal jurisdiction varies according to subject matter and geographic location. The division of power between the federal and state governments is governed by the principle of federalism, the parameters of which are set out in the U.S. Constitution. Article I, Section 8 of the Constitution lists the "enumerated powers" of the federal government that were delegated to it by the states: the powers that the U.S. Congress may exercise, subject to the Bill of Rights and other safeguards within the Constitution. Any powers that are not expressly delegated to the federal government remain in the hands of the individual states or the "people."

Jurisdiction can be exclusive (when held entirely by a single authority) or concurrent (when shared between multiple authorities). For example, the federal government has exclusive jurisdiction over the question of who qualifies for U.S. citizenship; states no longer have any authority to make decisions about citizenship. In situations of concur-

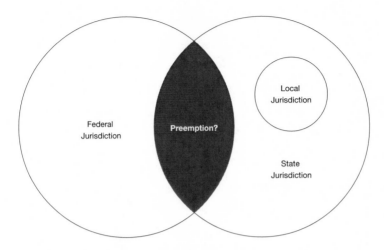

Figure 1. Federal and State Jurisdictions in the United States.

rent jurisdiction, authority is shared between multiple levels of government. In such cases, both federal and state actors may be able to act concurrently, or may share different tasks with respect to the same issue. In some cases, an actor can be preempted from acting once another has legislated on a specific issue. States, for example, are generally preempted from passing laws that would set air pollution standards at any level less stringent than those already set by federal law. When state and federal law conflict in an area where the federal government has jurisdiction, the Supremacy Clause of the Constitution clarifies that federal law preempts state law (figure 1).[4]

The term *environment* is not mentioned in the U.S. Constitution. There is, therefore, no enumerated power of the federal government that deals explicitly with the environment. Yet the federal government plays a major role in American environmental law and policy, in large part because courts have interpreted many environmental issues as falling within the scope of enumerated powers that are indirectly related to the environment. The most important of these in modern U.S. environmental law is the interstate Commerce Clause, a constitutional provision

(Paragraph continues on p. 16)

SPOTLIGHT 2. INDIGENOUS PEOPLES

The U.S. Constitution refers to indigenous peoples as "Indians," a term tracing back to early European explorers' false belief that, in making contact with North America, they had reached the Indian subcontinent. Although the term *Native Americans* is often thought to be more respectful and less likely to create confusion with persons of Asian-Indian descent, the term *Indians* or *American Indians* continues to be used in many legal contexts.

CURRENT STATUS

Federal "Indian law"—U.S. law regarding indigenous peoples—is complex and in many cases differs from tribe to tribe. U.S. law recognizes many American Indian tribes as distinct political bodies who retain inherent powers of self-government, particularly within their own lands. At the same time, federal Indian law presumes that the U.S. Congress retains the power to modify or even eliminate indigenous powers of self-government. The tension between recognizing the sovereignty of indigenous peoples and presuming that the U.S. government has the authority to limit that sovereignty creates ongoing controversy in the field of federal Indian law.

HISTORICAL CONTEXT

Between 1789 and 1871, as the fledgling U.S. government expanded westward across North America, the U.S. government entered into hundreds of treaties with Indian tribes. Many of these treaties touched on environmental issues, including land use, hunting, and fishing. Over time, the U.S. government broke, altered, and/or honored many of these treaties. As a result, modern Indian treaty rights comprise a complex (and controversial) mosaic that can be difficult even for specialists to navigate.

During the 1800s, the U.S. government pursued an active policy of displacing Indians from their tribal lands, a policy accomplished in part through treaty making and in part through the Indian Removal

Act of 1830. An important modern artifact of this policy is the existence of more than three hundred land areas, commonly called "reservations," within the United States, which are reserved for a tribe or
tribes. Although Indian reservations are treated as permanent tribal
homelands, the policy of forced relocation during the nineteenth century means that many tribes' reservations are in fact far from their
ancestral land.

RESERVATIONS

The U.S. government holds title to the land in Indian reservations
(which covers some fifty-six million acres or more) but considers the
land to be held "in trust" on behalf of the tribe. Importantly, tribal trust
land is not governed by state law, though it is subject to federal law.
Today there are almost six hundred federally recognized indigenous
tribes in the United States, a third of which are in the state of Alaska.

RELATIONSHIP TO U.S. ENVIRONMENTAL LAW

The quasi-sovereign status of Indian tribes makes the relationship
between environmental and tribal law particularly complicated.
Since 1984, the Environmental Protection Agency has recognized
tribal governments as the primary parties for setting standards,
making environmental policy decisions, and managing environmental programs on Indian reservations—though all such actions are
still required to comply with federal statutes and regulations.

Many tribes have traditional understandings of the appropriate
relationship between humans and the environment that are different from, or even in tension with, U.S. federal policy. While generally
U.S. federal law applies to reservations and to individual American
Indians, some specific laws make exceptions for some tribal beliefs
and policies. For example, the so-called "eagle feather law" excepts
individuals of certifiable American Indian ancestry from wildlife
laws protecting eagles and other migratory birds, allowing individual Indians and tribes to continue traditional spiritual and cultural
practices, in which feathers play an important role.

that allows the federal government to adopt laws related to interstate commerce.[5] This provision has been used as the constitutional basis for most modern federal environmental laws—for example, those addressing air and water pollution.[6] Other constitutional provisions with environmental implications include the Property Clause, which has been used to justify environmental regulations affecting public lands,[7] and the treaty power, which gives the federal government the power to make treaties, and thus also to enact legislation implementing international agreements.[8]

Federalism allows for variability across legal regimes, as state law varies across states. This has benefits as well as disadvantages. For instance, a benefit of variation across state laws is that states can serve as "laboratories" for testing different approaches to (comparable) legal problems. State-based variation can also accommodate a variety of citizen preferences on how to balance conflicting interests on difficult issues. For example, while the U.S. Constitution does not mention the environment, a few state constitutions do provide their residents with environmental rights.[9] At least in theory, such variation offers people the option to choose to live in a state whose environmental law best fits their personal preferences. It also means that states can look to their neighbors for ideas on how they might best regulate the environment.

Although it offers some benefits, variation in environmental laws can also generate problems. If pollution laws vary from state to state, companies may choose to move to a state with lax standards, which can result in more pollution and lower environmental quality in that state, and present the potential for unfair economic competition with other states. This competition could then lead other states to also adopt more lenient laws in response, resulting in lower environmental quality overall—an environmental "race to the bottom." In these cases, having one federal standard may prevent negative legal competition between states. More generally, the mere existence of diverging laws creates costs for companies and individuals who have to find out about—and adhere to—a different set of laws every time they cross a state border.

This can negatively influence interstate trade and thus sometimes provides grounds for federal action under the Commerce Clause.

Like federal powers, the powers of local governments (including counties, municipalities, and cities) depend on the delegation of state power. In some states, the authority of local governments is regulated by the principle of home rule. Under home rule, local governments are allowed to pass any law they see fit within the constraints of state and federal law. In other states, local governments may act only when the power to do so has been expressly delegated to them by the state. Regardless of the model adopted by a specific state, environmental law is a difficult subject for local government, as even the most "local" environmental problems, such as stormwater runoff through a town's roadways, may affect surrounding areas—a matter of externalities. It may also be beyond the administrative or technical capacity of the local government to deal with particularly complex environmental issues.

FUNCTIONAL SEPARATION: LEGISLATIVE, EXECUTIVE, AND JUDICIAL BRANCHES

To prevent excessive concentration of power, the U.S. government was designed as a tripartite system, composed of three branches: the legislature, the executive, and the judiciary. The U.S. Constitution, which lays out the fundamental structure of the federal government, gives each of these branches power over some legal tasks (figure 2). State constitutions create similar structures for state governments. The segregation of branches ensures a separation of powers and allows for each branch to act as a check and balance on the others.

The legislature is responsible for the creation of laws. At the federal level, the legislature—collectively "Congress"—is constituted by the Senate and the House of Representatives. The Senate consists of two Senators from each state, while seats in the House are apportioned by the population of each state. So, while the most populous state (California) has

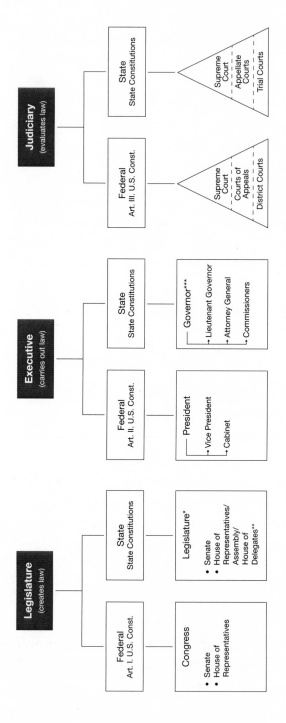

* In 25 states, the legislature is referred to as the "(State) Legislature." Other states use the terms "General Assembly," "General Court," and "Legislative Assembly."
** All states, except Nebraska, have a bicameral system composed of an upper house (Senate) and lower house (House of Representatives, etc.).
*** The composition of the state executive varies from state to state and may include these actors (and several more).

Figure 2. Structure of the U.S. Government.

fifty-three Representatives in the House, the least populous (Wyoming) has only one. But both states have the same number of Senators (two).

Legislators are directly elected by the people of their state. Senators are elected for a six-year term, while Representatives are elected for only two years. Legislators are often (but not always) reelected at the end of their term.

A key function of the legislature is to draft bills, which must be voted into law by both houses of Congress (that is, by the House and the Senate), and signed by the President, to become law. Laws passed in this way are called statutes. The vast majority of state legislatures are also composed of two separate legislative bodies with similar structures.[10]

The executive branch, headed by the President, is tasked with implementing and enforcing the law. The President is elected by the people of the United States.[11] In turn, the President is responsible for nominating members of the Cabinet, who are then presented to the Senate for confirmation. Cabinet members with important environmental roles include the Secretary of the Interior, the Secretary of Agriculture, the Secretary of Health and Human Services, the Attorney General, and the Secretary of Energy. Similarly, the President is responsible for hiring (and, if necessary, firing) most heads of administrative agencies, including the Environmental Protection Agency (EPA). The President thus has significant authority over many agencies. Most states have similar structures for their executive branches, although the head of a state executive branch is called a Governor.

Finally, the judiciary is empowered to interpret the law—to "say what the law is"—and to ensure that constitutional limits are respected. Courts play an important role in reviewing agency actions to ensure that agencies have acted constitutionally and within the scope of their statutory authority. In addition, as discussed further in chapter 3, the United States is a common law system, in which courts make decisions on the basis of custom and judicial precedent. This means that judicial decisions are binding on future litigants, and act as their own source of law.[12]

In the United States, there are two largely separate judicial systems: the federal judiciary and state judiciaries. Generally speaking, the federal judiciary is responsible for interpreting federal law, and state judiciaries are responsible for interpreting state law. State common law continues to play a particularly important role at the intersection of environmental law and areas traditionally reserved to state authority, such as property law and criminal law.

U.S. court systems are hierarchical. Parties must typically begin by filing their cases with trial courts, called "district courts" at the federal level and often called "trial courts" at the state level. Courts at the trial level are responsible for finding facts and for making initial determinations of the relevant law. After a trial court resolves the case, either of the parties may choose to appeal the decision of the trial court to the appellate court, called "the U.S. Courts of Appeals" at the federal level. Appellate courts generally defer to lower courts for factual questions but may overrule the lower court on questions of law. Parties displeased with the outcome at the appellate level may then seek an additional level of review, in a state supreme court, or in the U.S. Supreme Court, although review at this level is left to the discretion of the nine Supreme Court Justices.

The United States' tripartite system is aimed at ensuring a process of checks and balances among the three branches. In principle, all three branches are meant to be distinct in function and personnel: all branches fulfill different roles, and typically no person holds office in more than one branch.[13] There are many ways in which the system tries to prevent any of its branches from becoming too powerful or from acting outside of their democratic mandates. For example, the President may veto a law passed by Congress, but this veto can be overridden with a vote of two-thirds of both the Senate and the House. The President, subject to approval by the Senate, appoints all federal judges. Yet those same judges can limit executive authority if the President steps outside the limits of the Constitution.

At the state level, the same tripartite division exists, mirroring the federal system. State branches operate in parallel to, and at times overlap with, the federal branches. For example, in many environmental contexts, the federal government issues laws and regulations that govern an environmental issue but leaves implementation and enforcement up to the individual states. Similarly, the relationship between the state and federal courts is not a purely hierarchical one, but rather one of generally separate spheres of influence. State courts are shaped by the constitutions of their respective states, which means that states can have different rules regarding the structure of their court system. In contrast to the federal court system, state judges may be appointed or elected, depending on the state. The jurisdiction of state courts is exclusive in cases that involve only state law or state constitutional law—for example, most cases involving family or criminal law. However, even these cases may be heard in the federal court system if the litigants are located in more than one state, or if federal law is affected. Finally, because of the Supremacy Clause, when federal courts believe a state law violates the U.S. Constitution, the federal courts may set aside the state law.

THE FOURTH BRANCH? ADMINISTRATIVE AGENCIES IN U.S. LAW

Administrative agencies are units of government created by statute. The role of U.S. administrative agencies has grown steadily over the past decades, and as discussed further in chapter 5, few Americans realize that federal administrative agencies are now responsible for issuing more binding rules of conduct than Congress, and for adjudicating more disputes than all federal courts combined. Approximately $1 trillion per year is spent to comply with federal regulations—about one-tenth of the gross domestic product of the United States. And even these figures fail to capture the full impact of administrative regulation in the country, given that most states, as well as some counties and municipalities, also create and rely upon their own agencies.

The relationships of agencies to the three branches of government are shown in figure 3. In most cases, the legislature places agencies under the

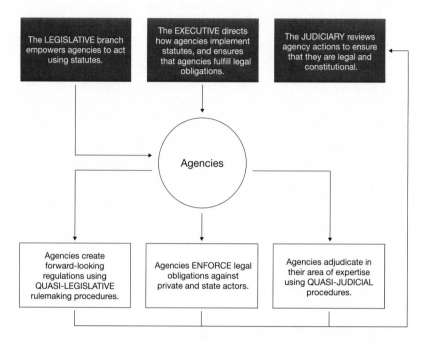

Figure 3. Relationships between Administrative Agencies and the Three Branches.

authority of the executive branch.[14] This means that the executive has significant control over enforcing agency functions, including through the hiring and firing of agency heads. Actions by agencies in passing rules or adjudicating disputes are reviewable by the judicial branch, except where the legislature chooses to limit judicial review. Courts routinely review agency action to determine whether the agency has acted within the bounds of the Constitution and of the agency's statutory authority. The agency must also adequately explain its reasoning; if it does not, the court may overturn the agency's decision for being "arbitrary and capricious."

A number of key agencies play a particularly important role within U.S. environmental law (see spotlight 3). At the federal level, the most important of these is the EPA. In addition, each state and territory has at least one environmental agency, and many states have several.[15] Pennsyl-

---

SPOTLIGHT 3. ENVIRONMENTAL AGENCIES

The Environmental Protection Agency (EPA) plays a central role in creating, enforcing, and administering the environmental law of the United States. But it is not the only federal agency tasked with environmental functions. Agencies other than the EPA with important statutory authority over environmental issues include the following:

- Department of Agriculture (agriculture), which also includes the U.S. Forest Service (management of national forests)
- Department of Energy (energy policy and conservation)
- Department of Justice (environmental crimes)
- Department of the Interior (resource management and endangered species), which includes the Fish and Wildlife Service (fish and wildlife management), the Bureau of Land Management (administration of public lands), and the National Park Service (management of national parks)
- National Highway Traffic Safety Administration (fuel economy standards)
- National Oceanic and Atmospheric Administration (marine resources and atmospheric research)
- Occupational Safety and Health Administration (occupational health risks)

---

vania, for example, has a Department of Environmental Protection and a Department of Conservation and Natural Resources, as well as a Department of Health that deals with environmental human health impacts.

Understanding agency action often requires the simultaneous navigation of multiple statutes and background legal norms. Regulations issued by administrative agencies are created through the agency actions of rulemaking or adjudication, rather than through legislation, and are restricted to the scope of authority delegated to the relevant

TABLE 2

Important Environmental Statutes Administered by the Environmental
Protection Agency

Statute	Year(s)	Topic
Clean Air Act (CAA)	1970/1990	Air pollution
Clean Water Act (CWA)	1972/1977	Water pollution
Federal Insecticide, Fungicide and Rodenticide Act (FIFRA)	1973	Useful poisons
Safe Drinking Water Act (SDWA)	1974	Drinking water quality
Toxic Substances Control Act (TSCA)	1976/2016	Toxic substances
Comprehensive Environmental Response, Compensation, and Liability Act (CERCLA) ("Superfund")	1980/1986	Hazardous waste
Resource Conservation and Recovery Act (RCRA)	1984/1986	Solid waste

agency by statute. Most importantly, however, agencies must be understood in light of the statutes that give them power.

A number of important environmental statutes give the EPA particularly broad authority over a wide range of environmental issues (table 2).[16]
These include many of the most important pollution control statutes,
such as the Clean Air Act and the Clean Water Act.

Additional statutes apply environmental requirements to many
other agencies. For example, under the National Environmental Policy
Act, since 1970, every federal agency has been required to assess and
disclose the significant environmental impacts of its undertakings.[17]
Because statutes are difficult and time-consuming to change, these
requirements tend to be durable.

As with the EPA, a single agency can be responsible for administering
multiple statutes. Similarly, as with the National Environmental Policy

Act, a single statute may be implemented by multiple agencies. A single agency can also be responsible for engaging in all three functions typically associated with all three branches of government. Statutes often direct agencies to act like legislatures by drafting legally binding rules through the process of rulemaking. Under the Clean Air Act, for example, the EPA is required to issue rules to set National Ambient Air Quality Standards, which set maximum levels for important air pollutants. In other contexts, agencies are directed to act like the executive by enforcing existing laws. For example, the Comprehensive Environmental Response, Compensation, and Liability Act empowers the EPA to initiate enforcement actions against the owners of toxic waste sites, and to order cleanup of those sites. Finally, agencies are often required to act like the judiciary by adjudicating disputes that arise under a statute. For example, Congress has given the EPA the primary responsibility for interpreting the Resource Conservation and Recovery Act. Under that Act, an administrative law judge at the EPA is empowered to impose penalties where solid waste disposal rules have been violated.

The role of regulatory agencies within U.S. law is often understood to present a tension between technical expertise and democratic accountability. The heads of most agencies, who have significant authority in setting priorities for agency decision making, are political appointees of the President (and can be removed by the President for political reasons). But while these four thousand appointees may be politically accountable through the President, the other two million employees of federal agencies are civil servants who are not elected and cannot be removed from their positions for political reasons. Most agency personnel are therefore relatively insulated from the types of political pressures that weigh upon legislatures and the executive. This allows agencies to develop technical expertise that can be particularly valuable when managing complex issues such as those that arise in environmental law. On the other hand, political insulation arguably reduces the democratic accountability of agencies, which may be particularly worrisome when agency action implicates important social values.

ENFORCEMENT

Federal environmental laws may be enforced against violators through three mechanisms: administrative enforcement actions, civil enforcement actions, and criminal enforcement actions. Of these three mechanisms, administrative and criminal enforcement actions are brought by government actors, whereas civil enforcement action may be initiated by either government or private actors.

Agencies generally have broad discretion in choosing when and how to bring administrative enforcement actions. Agencies may require violators to engage in (or stop engaging in) specific behaviors, and may also assess monetary penalties. Civil penalties for violating environmental laws can be significant: violation of the Clean Air Act, for example, can result in fines of up to $100,000 per violation, per day.[18] In addition, many environmental statutes provide for criminal prosecution by the Department of Justice. Such cases are administered through the judicial system, and may result in a monetary fine paid to the U.S. Treasury, or even in incarceration. While criminal prosecution for the violation of environmental laws is rare, the threat of criminal prosecution is often thought to act as a deterrent to potential violators.

As a backstop to administrative enforcement, most major U.S. environmental statutes also include provisions for so-called citizen suits, which grant "any person" the right to sue to enforce legal obligations (see spotlight 4). Such civil suits, managed through the judicial system, may result in injunctive relief, civil penalties, or both.

BEYOND THE UNITED STATES:
THE ROLE OF INTERNATIONAL LAW

Environmental processes are not limited by jurisdictional boundaries and can therefore affect, and be affected by, actions beyond U.S. borders. The most salient example of this type of interaction can be found in climate change. Human activity, particularly the emission of green-

SPOTLIGHT 4. CITIZEN SUITS AND STANDING

Most U.S. environmental statutes—with the notable exception of the National Environmental Policy Act (NEPA)—provide for "citizen suits" as a mechanism for enforcement. Citizen suits are lawsuits that can be brought by "any person," including interested private citizens. Citizen suits may be brought against private violators of a statute—for example, a community group may bring a citizen suit to directly enforce the terms of the Clean Water Act against a factory that is dumping waste into a local waterway. Alternatively, citizen suits can be brought against an agency that is failing in its enforcement responsibilities.

Although citizen suits theoretically provide an enforcement backstop for environmental laws, all citizen suits—including those under environmental law—are subject to minimum "standing" requirements. Standing doctrine attempts to ensure that judicial cases address a "case or controversy" that is appropriately reviewable by a court—a constitutional requirement under Article III of the U.S. Constitution. Judicial reasoning in this area is complex, and infamously puzzling even to advanced students of U.S. law. As a general matter, however, standing rules attempt to ensure that persons bringing a claim have experienced a particularized injury that was caused by something that the court can meaningfully redress. This requirement has proven to be a barrier for addressing many common environmental harms, such as the loss of endangered species or the risks of climate change, which accrue equally to all citizens and therefore do not fulfill the criterion of a "particularized" injury.

house gases, has set in motion a chain of environmental events that are culminating in permanent changes in global climate. The full effects of climate change are not yet visible and vary across the globe. Similarly, many actors have contributed to the causes of climate change. This combination of causal complexity and diffuse nonhuman effects characterizes climate change as a quintessential environmental problem. At the same time, it can be distinguished from "traditional" environmental problems by the the global scope of its causes and effects, which makes it difficult for any one country to address alone. The example of climate change highlights the importance of understanding the position of the United States as an international actor in environmental regulation. This necessitates exploring the powers of the United States in the international arena, as well as the reception of international law within the United States.

International law is distinct from national law in several ways. First, international law is the exclusive domain of nation states; individuals can derive rights from international law only as the subject of a national government. For example, while an individual cannot be a party to an international human rights treaty, she or he can invoke human rights by virtue of being a citizen of a country that is party to such a treaty.[19] Second, and relatedly, international law cannot be enforced in the same way as national law. An individual who breaches domestic law can be sentenced to a fine or imprisonment by a national court—in the United States, a federal or state court. A nation state that breaches international law cannot be sanctioned in the same way. Even when countries accept the jurisdiction of international courts or the obligations imposed by international treaties, there is no separate body capable of enforcing the resulting judgment or agreement: if a country refuses to pay the fine that may have been imposed, for example, its possessions cannot be confiscated nor can its representatives be sent to jail. The United Nations—the most important international organization, with near-universal membership—can impose certain sanctions on countries, but even these are difficult to enforce, and not necessarily based on the infringement of international law. As of this writing, the United States, a member of the United Nations Security Council, has never been subject to any kind of UN enforcement action.

There are several international courts of law, such as the International Court of Justice (ICJ), but their jurisdictions are restricted.[20]

When a country wishes to bring a case against another country before the ICJ, both nations have to consent to its jurisdiction, which often does not happen. Historically, the United States has been particularly reluctant to accept the jurisdiction of international courts, including the ICJ.[21]

The United States has also chosen not to join a number of otherwise-influential international environmental treaties, including the Convention on the Law of the Sea and the Convention on Biological Diversity—though it has joined others, including the Montreal Protocol on Substances that Deplete the Ozone Layer and the Convention on International Trade in Endangered Species of Wild Fauna and Flora. It is also a party to several multilateral environmental agreements, particularly with Canada, including the Migratory Birds Treaty and the Great Lakes Water Quality Agreement. While the United States is a party to the United Nations Framework Convention on Climate Change, it has refused to join international agreements (such as the Kyoto Protocol or the Paris Agreement) that would require it to reduce its greenhouse gas emissions.

In considering why the United States joins fewer international treaties than many other nations, it can be helpful to understand the internal legal process necessary for the United States to join a treaty. Under the Constitution, the President of the United States is empowered to unilaterally sign treaties with foreign nations. For these treaties to become binding on the U.S. government, however, the signature needs to be approved by a two-thirds majority of the Senate (a process known as ratification).[22] Different Presidents often have different policy positions, and if an agreement is signed by one President but not ratified by the Senate, a subsequent President can unilaterally reverse course. Somewhat famously, this is what occurred after President Obama signed the Paris Agreement in 2016; the Senate failed to ratify, and President Obama's successor, President Trump, withdrew support from the agreement.

If a treaty is *both* signed and ratified, it generally becomes part of U.S. domestic law. However, the Supreme Court has held that some international law is not "self-executing" and therefore needs to be separately implemented via statute.[23] Individuals who want to bring a case before a domestic court on the basis of international law can only do so on the basis of international law that has become part of domestic law, either through statute or by being self-executing.

The states have no well-defined role to play in international law, as the power of the President to enter into treaties is exclusive. That said, when the President fails to enter into a treaty, or the Senate refuses to ratify, states may decide to take action on their own accord in line with international law. This cannot bind the U.S. government but is typically permitted unless it undermines the United States' collective position.[24] For example, although the United States has domestic programs related to climate change, as we discuss further in chapter 8, it has not ratified most important international treaties on climate change. This has led many municipalities to sign on to the Mayors Climate Protection Agreement, which urges federal and state governments to act on climate change.

The United States is an important actor in international law due to its economic, military, and cultural authority. While it is a party to some international environmental agreements, U.S. environmental policy is still largely determined by domestic law and unilateral domestic action.

SUMMARY

The question of who creates, implements, enforces, and interprets U.S. environmental law can be as complex and important as the question of what constitutes U.S. environmental law. This chapter has provided an overview of the relationship between federal, state, and local governments, the structure of the branches of U.S. government, and the process of administrative regulation. These institutions, and the interaction between them, provide the institutional structure on which U.S. environmental law is built.

TAKEAWAYS

✓ The federal structure of the United States divides jurisdiction among multiple levels of government. The federal government has only those powers enumerated in the U.S. Constitution; generally, these powers are interpreted to include many aspects of environmental law. Authority not granted to the federal government is reserved to the states, which often choose to delegate power to local governments.

✓ The U.S. governmental system functions through three separate branches: the legislative, the executive, and the judiciary. The interaction between these branches is regulated through a system of checks and balances, which limits concentration of power.

✓ Administrative agencies also play a critical role in creating, enforcing, and evaluating U.S. law. Within environmental law, the Environmental Protection Agency is a key actor.

✓ U.S. environmental law is enforced through administrative, civil, and/or criminal enforcement actions.

✓ U.S. environmental law is influenced by, and influences, international action on environmental issues. That said, the United States continues to regulate environmental impacts primarily through domestic rather than international law.

KEY TERMS

ACTS Laws created by a federal or state legislature (aka *statutes*).

AGENCIES Units of government created by statute.

BILLS Legislative proposals that have not yet been voted on by the legislature.

CHECKS AND BALANCES A model of governance that limits the concentration of power by giving each of the branches of government the authority to limit the power of the other(s).

CITIZEN SUIT A lawsuit brought by a private citizen to enforce the law.

COMMERCE CLAUSE Clause of the U.S. Constitution that allows the federal government to regulate issues that (may) affect foreign or interstate trade.

EXECUTIVE ORDERS Legal directives created by the President to execute law.

EXTERNALITIES Costs or benefits created by an activity that are experienced by parties other than the one engaged in the activity.

FEDERALISM System (and principle) of government in which several states form a union for some purposes while remaining independent for others.

(GOVERNMENTAL) FUNCTION Responsibilities and powers of government, in the United States, as fulfilled by three branches of government: the legislature, executive, and judiciary.

JURISDICTION The authority to make legally binding decisions within a given territory or subject area.

PREEMPTION A process whereby the law of one level of government displaces the law of another. In the United States, this is most commonly preemption of state law by federal law.

PRIVATE ACTORS Individuals, nongovernmental organizations, or companies acting in their own interest (and not on behalf of the government).

PUBLIC ACTORS Members of government, or those acting on behalf of the government in an official capacity.

RACE TO THE BOTTOM Process whereby (environmental) standards are continually lowered to remain competitive with other jurisdictions.

RATIFICATION Approval of a signed international treaty by Congress.

REGULATIONS Binding rules of legal conduct issued by agencies; may also refer to the action or process, by any legal actor, of limiting or encouraging patterns of behavior.

SEPARATION OF POWERS An organizational principle of government whereby the legislative, executive, and judicial functions of the government are assigned to separate actors.

STATUTES Laws created by a federal or state legislature (aka *acts*).

DISCUSSION QUESTIONS

1. Do you think the balance of power between the federal and state governments in the United States makes sense? From a political perspective? From the perspective of managing environmental impacts?

2. What do you think of the role of agencies in U.S. environmental law? What do you consider the main strengths and weaknesses of using agencies in addressing environmental problems?

3. Are there any actors that you think should play a bigger role in U.S. environmental law?

4. With which actor in U.S. environmental law are you most familiar? Why?

5. Should the President play a larger or smaller role in U.S. environmental law?

6. What do you think about the role of international law in U.S. environmental law?

NOTES

1. Private actors—individual citizens, companies, and non-governmental organizations—also play an important part in environmental law. In the United States, for example, private actors often have the power to bring lawsuits, both to address private wrongs and to enforce federal statutes. We discuss several of these powers further in chapter 3. That said, one key power of individual citizens is to elect public representatives at the federal, state, and local levels.

2. The U.S. Fish and Wildlife Service maintains a list of resources addressing the relationship between the United States and tribal governments at https://www.fws.gov/nativeamerican/laws.html.

3. Under Article IV, Section 3 of the federal Constitution, candidates for statehood must gain approval from the U.S. Congress. The most recent states to join the union were Alaska and Hawaii, both admitted in 1959. Political movements to add additional states—particularly in Puerto Rico and the District of Columbia—have gained some traction in recent years.

4. U.S. CONST. art. VI, § 2 (establishing that the Constitution, federal laws made pursuant to it, and treaties made under its authority constitute the "supreme Law of the Land").

5. U.S. CONST. art. I, § 8, clause 3 (stating that the federal government shall have power "To regulate Commerce with foreign Nations, and among the several States, and with the Indian Tribes").

6. The Supreme Court, for example, has described the Commerce Clause as "broad enough to permit congressional regulation of activities causing air or water pollution, or other environmental hazards that may have effects in more than one State." *Hodel v. Virginia Surface Mining & Reclamation Association, Inc.,* 452 U.S. 264, 282 (1981).

7. See U.S. CONST. art. IV, § 3 (giving the U.S. Congress the power to "make all needful Rules and Regulations respecting" the property of the United States). For example, in *Kleppe v. New Mexico,* 426 U.S. 529 (1976), the Property Clause was relied upon to sustain the Wild Free-Roaming Horses and Burros Act of 1971 as a "needful regulation" "respecting" public lands," despite the State of New Mexico's argument that the federal government lacked the authority to control animals outside interstate commerce.

8. See U.S. CONST. art. II, § 2 (providing that the President "shall have Power, by and with the Advice and Consent of the Senate, to make Treaties, provided two-thirds of the Senators present concur"). For example, in *Missouri v. Holland,* U.S. (1920), the Supreme Court sustained the federal government's authority to implement the Migratory Bird Act of 1918, which implemented a treaty between the United States and Great Britain (acting on behalf of Canada) to protect migratory birds, on the basis of the treaty power.

9. The Illinois constitution, for example, provides that "[t]he public policy of the State and the duty of each person is to provide and maintain a healthful environment for the benefit of this and future generations." ILL. CONST. art. XI. Other states that provide a state constitutional right to a clean environment include Montana, Hawaii, Massachusetts, Pennsylvania, and Rhode Island.

10. The State of Nebraska is the sole exception: it has only a single legislative body.

11. The election of the President remains somewhat indirect, as the President is elected by members of the so-called Electoral College. Members of the

Electoral College have the technical authority to vote as they wish, but instances of members voting against public preference are extremely rare.

12. The common law system is discussed in more detail in chapter 3.

13. A rare example of overlap in personnel can be found in the Vice President, who is considered part of the executive branch but also holds the position of "President of the Senate." In the latter capacity, the Vice President is allowed to vote in case of a tie between the one hundred Senate members.

14. Occasionally, the legislature opts instead to create independent agencies, which are deliberately created outside of the oversight of the executive. For example, the National Aeronautics and Space Administration (NASA) is an independent agency, and the President has only very limited authority over it.

15. The EPA maintains a master list; see www2.epa.gov/home/health-and-environmental-agencies-us-states-and-territories.

16. The Congressional Research Service has compiled a comprehensive list of environmental statutes administered by the EPA, available at https://fas.org/sgp/crs/misc/RL30798.pdf.

17. See National Environmental Policy Act (NEPA) of 1969, 42 U.S.C. §§ 4321–4370h (2018) and spotlight 11.

18. Most major federal statutes identify a maximum statutory penalty; such penalties are modified by the Debt Collection Improvement Act of 1996 to account for inflation.

19. The exception to this is international criminal law, which increasingly applies to individuals.

20. Most other international courts have a subject-matter-based jurisdiction (e.g., the International Criminal Court). Some courts are restricted further geographically or temporally (e.g., the International Criminal Tribunal for the former Yugoslavia).

21. Although generally reluctant to accept the jurisdiction of international courts, the United States has been part of some important international cases. See, e.g., Trail Smelter Arbitration (*United States v. Canada*), Arbitral Trib., 3 U.N. REP. INT'L ARB. AWARDS 1905 (1941).

22. As provided for in U.S. CONST. art. VI.

23. See, e.g., *Medellín v. Texas,* 552 U.S. 491 (2008).

24. For more discussion of the role of states and cities in international law, see Lesley Wexler, *Bringing International Law the Long Way Home: Subfederal Integration of Unratified and Unimplemented Treaty Law,* 28 MICH. J. INT'L L. 1 (2006).

CHAPTER THREE

Types of Law

This chapter sets out the types of U.S. law available to legal actors in creating, implementing, and enforcing environmental legal strategies.

Knowing about the different types of law that make up U.S. environmental law is valuable for several reasons. First, different types of laws are made through different processes and often involve different key actors. Understanding the process underlying different types of law can also be useful in predicting future laws, and in advocating legal change. Second, different types of law require different strategies for researching and understanding what the law is.

To understand U.S. environmental law, it is important to understand some basic facts about four types of law: common law, constitutional law, statutes, and regulations. Each of these types of law originates with different institutional actors, is made in a different way, and is subject to change in a different way as well. Perhaps unsurprisingly, approaches to researching and understanding different types of U.S. environmental law can differ, depending on which type or types of laws apply to the environmental issue in question.

LEGAL SYSTEMS AND U.S. COMMON LAW

What do we talk about when we talk about "law"? As a general matter, a law is a rule binding conduct. But who makes that law, who enforces it, and how can it change? The answers to these questions will vary depending on the "type" of law being considered.

One of the most important distinctions typically drawn between modern legal systems is between "common law" and "civil law" systems. The system a jurisdiction uses affects both how the law operates and how a citizen (or researcher) can find out what the law is. In civil law systems, such as those used in the majority of countries around the world (including most European countries and China), core legal principles are systematically codified into referable systems, or "codes." These are meant to essentially stand on their own, with court judgments serving only to clarify uncertain terms. This means that, in a civil law system, it is often possible to develop a reasonable understanding of the law by searching through the codes.

Common law systems, such as those in the United States, are different.[1] In common law systems, there is no comprehensive compilation of legal rules in a codified form. Even particular rules that have been at least partially codified—such as those found in constitutions, statutes, and regulations—are subject to interpretation by courts. In adjudicating cases, common law courts give precedential authority to prior court decisions and base their own decisions on judge-made common law principles that were developed in prior cases.

The common law system was originally developed in medieval England. Like most other former British colonies, upon declaring independence, the United States retained the common law system. Forty-nine of the fifty states also use a common law system.[2]

Because common law relies on lines of precedent created by judges, it is often necessary to read and interpret lines of precedential judicial opinions to understand what the law is likely to be in any particular scenario. This is a complicated task—so complicated that it is sometimes used to justify the fact that American attorneys are required to earn a graduate degree in law, rather than the undergraduate degree that suffices throughout much of the world. In any case, to simplify the task of interpreting the law, lawyers in the United States often rely on "treatises," scholarly compendiums that attempt to accurately summarize the common law on particular topics. While these can be very useful aids to research, however, and can sometimes be persuasive to courts, they have no legal power on their own.

Judges play importantly different roles in civil law and common law systems. In civil law systems, judges act as investigators, and often take an active role in developing the judicial record. But they see their role as limited to understanding codified laws. In common law systems, judges tend to take a more hands-off, referee-style approach in the courtroom, allowing advocates to plead their case persuasively, and to take charge of investigation and argument. Because written judicial opinions generally carry precedential authority, in the United States, judges' opinions have substantial ability to shape the substance of environmental (and other) laws.

Like other common law courts around the world, U.S. courts view themselves as bound by precedent, in a principle known as *stare decisis* (Latin: "to stand by things decided"). According to the Supreme Court, courts apply stare decisis because it "promotes the evenhanded, predictable, and consistent development of legal principles, fosters reliance on judicial decisions, and contributes to the actual and perceived integrity of the judicial process."[3] U.S. courts thus defer to prior decisions from superior courts in similar cases—in a principle commonly called vertical stare decisis, or binding precedent. They also often defer to their own prior decisions, through horizontal stare decisis.[4] Even where not bound by precedent, U.S. federal and state courts often cite to the reasoning in similar cases from other U.S. jurisdictions that they find persuasive.

Even within common law systems, different types of law apply depending on whose behavior is being addressed by the law. "Private law" applies to private parties—for example, to individuals entering into contracts (governed by contract law) or individuals who harm other individuals (governed by tort law). "Public law," by contrast, applies to public actors acting in their public capacity, for example to regulators (whose behavior is governed by administrative law) or to legislators (whose ability to legislate is governed by the Constitution). Because the actions of private individuals and the actions of public servants can affect environmental quality, both private and public law can play important roles in regulating environmental quality.

SOURCES OF U.S. ENVIRONMENTAL LAW

Constitutional Law

Constitutional law is law that provides for the structure and functioning of the government—for how the government is "constituted." It can also involve descriptions of the rights that individuals have from and against their government. Constitutional law is public law.

The United States was the first country in the world to have a written constitution, and the U.S. Constitution remains both the oldest and the shortest national constitution in the world.[5] Unusually, the core of the Constitution has remained unchanged since it was drafted in 1787 and ratified in 1788. The structure of the U.S. government is described, briefly, in seven articles (see spotlight 5). One of these—Article V—describes how the Constitution can be amended.

Amending the federal Constitution is relatively burdensome.[6] Amendment requires a two-thirds majority vote in both the House of Representatives and the Senate (the method through which all twenty-seven amendments to the Constitution have been passed), or a constitutional convention called for by two-thirds of state legislatures (a method that has never yet been used). Either way, three-fourths of the states must affirm the proposed amendment. Despite this daunting set of requirements, proposals to amend the Constitution are common; the U.S. Senate estimates that there have been over 11,700 proposed amendments since

---

SPOTLIGHT 5. THE U.S. CONSTITUTION

The core of the U.S. Constitution, drafted in 1787, lays out the structure of the federal government.

Article I: Establishes and describes the powers of the legislative branch, including the House of Representatives and the Senate

Article II: Establishes and describes the powers of the executive branch, which is led by the President

Article III: Establishes and describes the powers of the judicial branch, which is empowered to review the constitutionality of laws and their execution

Article IV: Addresses the responsibilities, duties, and powers of the states

Article V: Addresses the process for amending the Constitution

Article VI: Establishes the Constitution as the "supreme law of the land," in a provision known as "the Supremacy Clause"

Article VII: Describes the process for ratifying the Constitution

---

1788.[7] But the burdensome procedures for ratification have helped keep successful amendment rare: in total, the Constitution has had only twenty-seven amendments. The first ten of these were adopted simultaneously in 1791 and have come to be known as the "Bill of Rights." These amendments were designed to list specific restrictions on governmental power and protections of personal liberties, including freedom of religion, speech, and assembly, and a guarantee of due process of law before being deprived of life, liberty, or property.

In the United States, when people refer to "the Constitution," they mean the federal U.S. Constitution. That said, each individual state has its own constitution as well. The state constitutions vary in substance, though they often mirror the structure of the U.S. Constitution.[8] Among the the fifty states, Massachusetts has the oldest constitution, adopted in 1780; in fact, it served as a model for the U.S. Constitution. The youngest state constitution is Rhode Island's, which was ratified by that state's voters in 1986 after a state constitutional convention. Most states have had more than one constitution since joining the United States; Louisiana has had the most, with eleven.

Article VII of the U.S. Constitution establishes the Constitution as the supreme law of the land. Thus, federal courts will overrule as "unconstitutional" any laws—federal or state common law, statutory law, or regulations—that are found to conflict with the federal Constitution. For example, if a federal statute is created that goes against a constitutional requirement—for example, by discriminating against protected groups as prohibited by the Fourteenth Amendment, or by attempting to regulate beyond the jurisdiction of the federal government—the courts will hold that statute invalid.

Unlike some more recently drafted constitutions around the world, the U.S. Constitution never explicitly mentions the environment.[9] And given that changes to the U.S. Constitution are burdensome and extraordinarily rare, it is unlikely that the explicit constitutional status of environmental protection will change any time in the near future.

Nevertheless, to be valid, all federal environmental laws must have a Constitutional basis for federal jurisdiction. Over the years, courts have interpreted general provisions of the Constitution as empowering Congress to regulate many environmental issues; among these, the most influential include the Commerce Clause, which allows the federal government "to regulate commerce with foreign nations, and among the several states, and with the Indian tribes," the Property Clause, and the treaty power.[10]

In some cases, the Constitution also acts as a limit on the federal government's power to effect environmental policies. For example, when government policies affect private property to the point that they are equivalent to the government "taking" the land, constitutional protections that prohibit the government from taking private property for public use may be triggered.[11]

Common Law

The U.S. common law tradition has resulted in an important role for the courts in creating and interpreting law. In the absence of codes, U.S. courts have developed doctrines to deal with similar types of cases. These doctrines are created by a series of judicial opinions that address similar facts.

Common law doctrines can apply to both private law and public law. As mentioned above, private law is law that governs relationships between individuals, rather than between individuals and the government. Someone who is harmed by a private party may bring suit as a plaintiff in a common law suit, against the party who caused the wrong (the defendant). If the plaintiff prevails, she may be awarded damages to compensate her for the harm caused by the defendant, and/or an injunction, a judicial order that requires the defendant to act (or not act) in a particular way.

Areas of private common law include contract law, property law, and tort law. Each of these areas of law can have important implications for environmental quality. For example, agreements to provide environmental services, such as waste management, are governed by contract law. Tort law and property law play an even more important role in regulating environmental quality. Tort law—the law of civil wrongs, which allows individuals to sue other individuals who have harmed them—is important for its role in regulating environmental risks to individuals. And property law plays a particularly important role in land-use decisions, as well as in the management of natural resources.

In the United States, private common law is traditionally governed by state rather than federal law. As a result, the specific rules and doctrines applied by courts tend to vary from state to state. Nevertheless, several particularly important doctrines in tort and property law apply in most states. Three common law tort doctrines that are particularly relevant to environmental cases are negligence, trespass, and nuisance (see spotlight 6).

SPOTLIGHT 6. IMPORTANT TORT DOCTRINES

NEGLIGENCE

The failure to satisfy a standard of reasonable care while perform-ing acts that foreseeably harm other people.

Example: A manufacturing facility that unreasonably failed to maintain chemical storage containers, leading to contamination of groundwater, could be liable in negligence for the cost of cleanup, and for any damages caused by the contamination.

TRESPASS

The intentional interference with the property interest of a property owner.

Example: A restaurant that purposely dumped its trash on a neighboring lot could be liable in trespass for the cost of cleanup, and for any damages caused by the dumping.

NUISANCE

The substantial and unreasonable interference with a property right. Nuisance doctrine commonly distinguishes between *private nuisance* and *public nuisance.*

Private Nuisance

A substantial and unreasonable interference with the private use and enjoyment of land.

Example: A newly built factory farm generating foul odors and noise could be liable in private nuisance to a neighboring property owner who was nauseated by the stench or unable to enjoy time outside because of the noise and smell.* Traditionally in the United

---

* Some states have "right to farm" statutes, which prohibit suits in nuisance against agricultural uses of land that has historically been used for agriculture. When these statutes apply, they generally overrule state common law on nuisance.

States, courts awarded injunctions to successful plaintiffs in nuisance suits. Modern U.S. courts now also consider damages as an alternative to injunction, up to the value of the interference with enjoyment of land.**

Public Nuisance

A substantial and unreasonable interference with the rights of the public.

Example: A copper smelter that caused acid rain and air pollution over a county-wide area could be sued in public nuisance, on behalf of all the members of the public affected by the pollution. Public nuisances commonly result in injunctions; if the smelter's behavior were unreasonable, it would likely be required to stop or curtail its smelting.

** Academics and courts continue a lively debate about when it is better policy to award injunctions, and when to grant damages. The modern practice of considering damages as an alternative to injunctions as a remedy in nuisance is often traced to the influential case of *Boomer v. Atlantic Cement Co.,* 287 N.Y.S.2d 112 (1967), in which a multimillion-dollar cement plant exposed its neighbors to serious noise and air pollution. The court held that the cement plant was a private nuisance, but granted the neighbors damages rather than an injunction to shut down the plant, because the cost of complying with an injunction would have been far more than the fair value of the cost to the plaintiffs of the cement plant continuing its operations.

Another type of torts that sometimes apply in environmental contexts are strict liability torts, particularly torts in product liability. Product liability torts arise when someone manufactures and/or distributes a product that causes harm to a person or property. In most U.S. jurisdictions, product liability is "strict" liability, because it arises even if the harm was not foreseeable, and even if the tortfeasor had no intent to harm. For example, manufacturers of lead paint in the United States have been held strictly liable in product liability for harm caused by the paint—particularly to children, who will often eat chips of the paint, which tastes sweet. Tort liability for abnormally dangerous activities, such as storing toxic waste or using explosives, is also strict. In general, lawsuits that involve toxic substances, and are based in tort law, are called "toxic torts."

Property law, which governs the legal relationships between people and things, is particularly relevant to environmental quality through its impact on land use and on people's use of natural resources. In the United States, landowners are subject to relatively few restrictions on their use of their land. They moreover enjoy constitutional protection under the Takings Clause from taking of private property for public use without just compensation. Some of the most important limitations on landowners' behaviors come from nuisance law (as described above), which prevents landowners from using their land in ways that unreasonably interfere with others' rights. Property rights are also constrained through zoning law, an administrative body of law that creates localized restrictions on building and use (see spotlight 7). Property law also offers a suite of legal tools that property owners can use to promote land uses with important environmental impacts. One of the most important of these is the creation of easements, which are rights to access or use land, often for a particular purpose or time period. In environmental law, conservation easements—voluntary legal agreements between landowners and a trust or government agency, which permanently limit use of the land to protect its conservation value— can play a valuable role in preserving local ecosystems and in promoting conservation. Conservation easements alone protect an estimated forty million acres of natural habitat, in part because of federal and state tax incentives.[12]

In addition to private common law, courts also administer public law doctrines. Public law is law that governs issues that affect the general public or state. Areas of public law include constitutional law, administrative law, and criminal law. These areas of law often involve several types of law: constitutional law, for example, obviously involves

---

SPOTLIGHT 7. ZONING

Zoning is the process of dividing land into "zones" in which certain land uses are either permitted or prohibited. Zoning was first practiced in the United States in the early twentieth century, and the practice of restricting land use with zoning has been held to be Constitutional by the Supreme Court.*

In the United States, zoning is primarily done by local (municipal) agencies, who set, enforce, and interpret zoning ordinances. Zoning restrictions routinely constrain how property owners may use their land. Building and construction restrictions can have important impacts on a number of local environmental quality issues, including soil erosion, storm water management and flooding, landscaping and tree preservation, and population density and traffic patterns.

Although zoning is almost universally practiced in municipalities throughout the United States, one notable exception to its common use is the city of Houston—the nation's fourth-largest city, with a population of 2.3 million—which famously has no zoning ordinances.

* See *Village of Euclid, Ohio v. Ambler Realty Co.* (1926).

---

constitutions, as well as common law interpretations of constitutional text. Similarly, administrative law routinely involves agency regulations, as well as common law doctrines governing the interpretation of regulations. Criminal law routinely involves both statutes and a series of common law doctrines that courts have developed to interpret those statutes. Constitutional law, regulations, and statutes are discussed in more detail below. For purposes of environmental law, perhaps the most important judicial doctrine is the *Chevron* doctrine, which governs how courts interpret regulatory statutes (see spotlight 8).

SPOTLIGHT 8. AGENCY DISCRETION AND
THE *CHEVRON* DOCTRINE

When it is unclear what a statute requires, who gets to decide what the statute means—courts or agencies? The Supreme Court took up this question in 1984, in the influential case of *Chevron v. Natural Resources Defense Council.* The case required the Court to evaluate the Environmental Protection Agency's interpretation of what counted as a "source" of air pollution under the Clean Air Act. While the statute had created far more stringent standards for "new or modified major stationary sources" of air pollution, the statute did not explain whether a "source" was a single smokestack or an entire facility (like an oil refinery, which might contain hundreds of smokestacks). The EPA, given general authority by Congress to regulate pursuant to the CAA, interpreted the statute as applying to entire facilities, rather than individual smokestacks. This interpretation was challenged by an environmental group, which argued that it violated the statute and would lead to degradation of air quality.

In its consideration of this question, the Supreme Court explained that, when a court reviews an agency's interpretation of a statute the agency administers, it faces two questions:

> First, always, is the question whether Congress has directly spoken to the precise question at issue. If the intent of Congress is clear, that is the end of the matter; for the court, as well as the agency, must give effect to the unambiguously expressed intent of Congress. If, however, the court determines Congress has not directly addressed the precise question at issue, the court does not simply impose its own construction on the statute, as would be necessary in the absence of an administrative interpretation. Rather, if the statute is silent or ambiguous with respect to the specific issue, the question for the court is whether the agency's answer is based on a permissible construction of the statute.

Applying this two-step approach, the Supreme Court held that the EPA had the discretion to adopt the facility-wide interpretation of the word *source*. The effect of this standard is that agencies have a great deal of power to interpret the statutes they administer. Courts step in to overrule agency interpretations only in rare circumstances, when Congress has "directly spoken to the precise question at issue" and told the agency to do the opposite of what it has done. Otherwise, courts will allow any reasonable statutory interpretation by an agency to stand—even if the court believes that there is another, better interpretation. This approach to evaluating agency authority has come to be known as the *Chevron* doctrine, and it is widely applied to environmental and other agency actions.

The *Chevron* doctrine has been highly influential in the creation of the modern regulatory state. That said, critics of *Chevron*—including several Supreme Court Justices—have expressed concern that *Chevron* may grant too much power to agencies, and that courts may need to increase the level of scrutiny with which they review agencies' statutory interpretations. If *Chevron* were weakened or overturned in the future, it could substantially change the amount of power that administrative agencies have to set environmental (and other) policy.

Statutes, Regulations, and Executive Orders

Apart from constitutional law and common law, laws created by the U.S. federal and state legislatures (statutes), and laws created by agencies (regulations) are crucial sources of U.S. environmental law. Executive orders—written directions from the President—also play an important role in influencing how agencies regulate.

STATUTES

In the United States, statutes—written laws enacted by legislatures—are created by legislatures at the federal level, and by legislatures or through direct democracy at the state level (see spotlight 9). The U.S.

(Paragraph continues on p. 50)

SPOTLIGHT 9. CREATION OF STATUTES

HOW ARE STATUTES MADE?

At the federal level, statutes must pass through multiple stages to become law. They begin when a bill—a piece of proposed legislation that has not yet become a statute—is proposed or sponsored by a legislator in either the House or the Senate. The bill goes to committee, where small groups of Representatives or Senators research, discuss, and amend the bill. If the committee votes to accept the bill, it is sent to the House or the Senate for debate and amendment. If the bill passes the first chamber, it is sent to the other to go through a similar process of committees, debate, and voting. Both the House and Senate must then agree to the same version of the final bill—a process known as reconciliation. The bill is then sent to the President, who can then approve or veto the bill. If it is approved, it becomes law.* Most state governments have a very similar legislative process, with the final say on the statute being provided by the governor. Some states also provide for direct democratic methods of creating statutes, using initiatives or referenda that place legal questions directly in front of state voters.

HOW CAN THEY BE CHANGED?

When a proposed statute is still in bill form, it can be changed by congressional committees or by the houses of Congress. Once the bill has become law, the legislature can change it only by enacting amendments, which might change some or all of the statute, or through rescission, both of which require substantially the same procedure as passing new legislation. Statutes can also be overruled by courts as unconstitutional, and state statutes can be preempted by federal statutes, in which case the federal law governs. Judicial interpretations of statutory terms can also change over time.

**HOW CAN I FIND OUT WHAT STATUTES SAY
ON A PARTICULAR TOPIC?**

All federal and state statutes are written down and published. Federal statutes are officially published in the United States Code (U.S.C.), and copies of federal statutes are widely available online. State statutes are frequently available on state websites.

---

* Many Americans are familiar with this legislative process in part through a famous (and remarkably accurate) song, "I'm Just a Bill," written for the 1970s children's educational program *Schoolhouse Rock*. The original video and song are widely available online, including at www.youtube.com/watch?v=FFroMQlKiag.

Congress, made up of the House of Representatives and the Senate, is responsible for passing federal statutes; state legislatures, organized according to state constitutions, pass state statutes. In some cases, states have also delegated authority to local (e.g., county or city) officials; when these officials pass statutes, those statutes are often called *ordinances*. Federal statutes may not violate the U.S. Constitution; state statutes may not violate the U.S. Constitution, the state constitution, or federal statutes (except where there is exclusive state jurisdiction).

Many of the most important U.S. environmental laws are federal statutes. These include the Clean Air Act, the Clean Water Act, the Endangered Species Act, and the National Environmental Policy Act. States often have their own environmental statutes as well. In some cases, these address similar environmental concerns as the key federal statutes; most states, for example, have their own environmental policy acts, and many also have air and water pollution statutes. State statutes and local ordinances also address a number of environmental topics not addressed by federal statutes, including local land management practices.

Generally speaking, when federal and state statutes address the same environmental issue, the federal statute is interpreted to create a minimum floor, but not a ceiling. In this case, states may choose to adopt more stringent environmental requirements than the federal standards would require, but they may not choose to adopt less stringent standards.

One feature of U.S. statutes that sometimes surprises outsiders is that they are often far more broadly written than statutes in many civil law countries. This can leave a number of ambiguities and potential grounds for disagreement about what the law is on any particular issue. Generally, the U.S. legal system manages these ambiguities through two methods. First, U.S. courts have the authority to say "what the law is" and to resolve statutory ambiguities. So, when there are disputes about what statutes mean, courts get the final word in interpretation—though the legislature can always amend the statute if it does not like how the court has interpreted it. Second, U.S. legislators often purposefully use statutes to create and delegate significant authority to administrative agencies. When that happens—as it often does in environmental cases—agencies then issue regulations (laws made by agencies), which typically provide more specific guidance about how the agency has interpreted the requirements of the statute.

REGULATIONS

Regulations are laws made by administrative agencies (see spotlight 10). In the United States, regulations include two types of agency action: rulemaking, or the creation of prospectively applicable general rules; and agency adjudication, where the agency formulates an order about more particularized facts. When agencies regulate by rulemaking, they must typically notify the public of the proposed rule, provide an opportunity for public comment, and consider submitted comments before publishing a final version of the rule in the Federal Register. When agencies adjudicate, they must follow any procedural requirements in the underlying statute, as well as due process and other constraints that follow from the Constitution. In some cases, they must also hold formal hearings. Agency adjudications are typically performed by Administrative Law Judges, who are agency employees.

SPOTLIGHT 10. CREATION OF REGULATIONS

HOW ARE REGULATIONS MADE?

Unless a specific statute directs otherwise, federal agencies must follow the procedures outlined in the Administrative Procedure Act. Most states have their own procedural rules for state agencies, often following the Model State Administrative Procedure Act. At both the federal and state levels, there are generally two types of procedure that agencies use in regulating: *rulemaking* and *adjudication*. Rulemaking involves setting general and prospectively applicable rules. Adjudication involves more particularized facts and may apply only to the parties before the agency.

HOW CAN REGULATIONS BE CHANGED?

Before most rulemakings are finalized, agencies must offer the public the opportunity to comment on the proposed rule. This provides an opportunity for commenters to participate in changing the rule before it becomes law. Once a regulation is final, it can often be challenged in court. The most common grounds for judicial challenge are that the agency exceeded the scope of its authority in passing the regulation, that the regulation is "arbitrary and capricious," that the agency failed to follow required procedures, and/or that the regulation is unconstitutional. Adjudications can be appealed within the agency or (sometimes) in court.

HOW CAN I FIND OUT WHAT REGULATIONS SAY ON A PARTICULAR TOPIC?

Notices of Proposed Rulemaking (NPRMs) are published in the Code of Federal Regulations, as are *final rules.* It can be more difficult to find agency adjudications, though agency websites publish some of them. States each maintain their own regulations; most publish these online.

Agencies are empowered to make regulations based on statutes that define their powers and responsibilities. Often, however, the statutory direction given to the agency is quite vague; to satisfy the Constitution, the statute only has to incorporate an "intelligible principle" through which the agency can regulate, and under *Chevron*, U.S. administrative agencies often have significant discretion to decide how to interpret and administer statutes, and have many options about which particular standards they will require through regulation. For example, when it drafted the Clean Air Act, Congress indicated that National Ambient Air Quality Standards (NAAQS) should be set for key air pollutants. The statute itself did not contain any actual limits for those pollutants, however; instead, it directed that NAAQS be set at the level "requisite to protect the public health" "with an adequate margin of safety." It then delegated to an agency—the Environmental Protection Agency—the power to determine what those levels of pollution should be. The EPA has subsequently issued a series of regulations setting NAAQS for key air pollutants, based on what it believes to be requisite to protect the public health with an adequate margin of safety.

Generally, federal agencies are also required to comply with the terms of the Administrative Procedure Act (APA), which provides the default requirements for the procedures that agencies follow in regulating. Among other requirements, the APA directs courts to overturn agency action that is "arbitrary, capricious, an abuse of discretion, or otherwise not in accordance with law" or that is "unsupported by substantial evidence." Courts also overturn agency regulations when they find that the regulation exceeds the agency's statutory authority, and where the regulation is found to violate the Constitution.

States also have their own agencies that issue regulations. Often, state and federal regulators work together to address common problems, and in fact many of the major federal environmental statutes allocate authority to both federal and state agencies. The Clean Air Act, for example, requires EPA to regulate to set NAAQS. But the statute delegates the primary authority to determine *how* the NAAQS will be met to states' agencies, which develop State Implementation Plans for achieving the NAAQS. The EPA then reviews the state plans for compliance with the statutory requirements, and typically works with the state agency to solve compliance challenges.

EXECUTIVE ORDERS

As the head of the executive branch, the President of the United States plays an important role in guiding agency discretion. Some of this guidance comes through informal means, such as the President calling the heads of administrative agencies to express a policy preference, or to threaten to fire the heads of agencies under executive direction, if they do not implement presidential preferences. Other mechanisms are more public. One particularly important mechanism for environmental law is the President's authority to issue executive orders, which are written directions from the President that are legally binding so long as they fall within the President's Constitutional authority. Presidents use executive orders for a wide range of purposes, ranging from declaring a new national holiday to giving specific directions to agencies on how to regulate in the absence of countervailing direction from the legislature. Since 1981, U.S. agencies have operated under a set of executive orders that centralize regulatory planning and review, and that direct them on how to address regulatory issues, including environmental issues. Other executive orders address environmental issues directly, as with Executive Order 11,990, encouraging the protection of wetlands; or Executive Order 12,898, directing agencies to consider the environmental justice impacts of their actions. While executive orders can be powerful, they are also subject to unilateral reversal by subsequent Presidents. For example, President Barack Obama issued an executive order in 2016 to adopt the Paris Agreement on Climate Change, but this order was reversed by Obama's successor, President Donald Trump.

SUMMARY

Different types of U.S. environmental law are created through different processes and by different actors. This affects their content, scope of application, and how they are interpreted by the courts.

TAKEAWAYS

✓ U.S. environmental law is affected by many types of U.S. law, including private and public law, law made at federal, state, and international levels, and incorporating statutes, judicial opinions, administrative regulations, and executive actions.

✓ Administrative regulations play a particularly important role in U.S. environmental law.

✓ Common law also affects U.S. environmental law, by "filling in the gaps" between environmental laws as written and the legal principles that underlie those laws.

✓ The effectiveness of U.S. environmental law relies on relationships between federal and state actors.

KEY TERMS

ADMINISTRATIVE LAW Law that governs administrative agencies.

ADMINISTRATIVE PROCEDURE Rules that govern procedures used by agencies and in agency proceedings.

CIVIL LAW A legal system that codifies core principles into referable systems, such as statutes.

CIVIL PROCEDURE The rules that must be followed in noncriminal judicial courts.

COMMON LAW Law made by judges, published in the form of judicial opinions, which gives precedential authority to prior court decisions (may be public or private law).

CONSTITUTIONAL LAW Law that provides for the structure and functioning of a government—for how the government is "constituted"—and how the government is supposed to interact with individuals (a form of public law).

CONTRACT LAW Law that governs how promises between individuals are enforced (a form of private law).

CRIMINAL LAW Law that governs the punishment and behavior of those who commit crimes—behaviors that are considered so socially damaging that they are punishable by law (a form of public law).

CRIMINAL PROCEDURE Rules that govern criminal legal procedures.

PRIVATE LAW Law that governs relationships between individuals (e.g., contract law, tort law, and property law).

PROPERTY LAW Law about the relationships between people and things.

PUBLIC LAW Law that governs issues that affect the general public or state (e.g., constitutional law, administrative law, and criminal law).

TORT LAW Law that governs how people can use law to redress harms or injuries that other individuals have caused them (a form of private law).

DISCUSSION QUESTIONS

1. Who is best positioned to make environmental law: judges, legislatures, agencies, the President, or some other actor?

2. Does it make sense to have a constitution that does not address the environment? Should the U.S. Constitution be amended to include the environment? If so, how?

3. Should criminal law play a role with respect to environmental impacts? What challenges do you see in using criminal law to regulate the environment?

4. How important is it for environmental law to be able to change quickly, in response to changing circumstances or improving information? Which type(s) of law are most likely to be able to respond quickly to changes, and which would you expect to be slower to change?

NOTES

1. Each state has its own common law, or in the case of Louisiana, a mixed system of civil and common law.

2. The exception is Louisiana, which developed its laws originally when it was a French colony and which continues to use a civil code based on the Napoleonic Code. That said, Louisiana's criminal law is mostly based on common law, which makes it a mixed legal system.

3. *Kimble v. Marvel Enterprises,* 135 S. Ct. 1697 (2015).

4. For example, a federal district court—which is a trial-level court—in Chicago is in the Seventh Federal District. That district court is bound by precedent set at the Seventh Circuit Court of Appeals—an example of binding precedent and of vertical stare decisis. Similarly, the district court is bound by the precedent of the U.S. Supreme Court. The district court has the authority to overrule its own prior precedent, but it generally will not: most of the time, it—like other courts—will follow its own precedent as per horizontal *stare decisis.* The federal district court is not bound to follow the precedent of any other federal district or circuit court—although it may find opinions from those courts highly persuasive.

5. The U.S. Constitution was ratified in 1788, at which point it was 4,400 words long. Including all its twenty-seven modern amendments, it has now reached 7,591 words in length. Compare this to the longest national constitution in the world—India's—which clocks in at 117,000 words.

6. State constitutions generally feature less restrictive amendment processes, and many provide for multiple avenues to constitutional change. These often provide for direct democratic participation—through constitutional initiatives, for example. In a constitutional initiative process, citizens can collect signatures on a petition to place a constitutional amendment on the ballot, for voters to then adopt or reject. Through these means, such states can have constitutional amendments without any direct involvement of either the Governor or members of the state legislature. For a description of state

constitutions and their amendment processes, see Marvin Krislov and Daniel Katz, *Taking State Constitutions Seriously*, 17 CORNELL J. L. & PUB. POL'Y 295 (2008).

7. The U.S. Senate keeps a record of the number of proposals for amendment on its website, available at www.senate.gov/legislative/MeasuresProposed ToAmendTheConstitution.htm.

8. Although it is common for state constitutions to mirror the U.S. Constitution, not all do so. The Alabama Constitution is one notable example. Drafted in 1901 and amended many times, the Alabama Constitution is 310,296 words long—forty-four times longer than the U.S. Constitution, and the longest constitution in the world.

9. Some state constitutions do explicitly address the environment or environmental concerns. Six states, for example—Illinois, Pennsylvania, Massachusetts, Hawaii, Montana, and Rhode Island—guarantee their citizens some kind of constitutional right to a clean environment.

10. U.S. CONST. art. I, § 8, clause 3; see infra pages 15–16. For a detailed overview of the development of the federal power to regulate the environment and its basis in the U.S. Constitution, see Robert V. Percival, *Greening the Constitution—Harmonizing Environmental and Constitutional Values,* 32 ENVTL. L. 809 (2002).

11. Robert Meltz, Dwight Merriam, and Rick Frank, THE TAKINGS ISSUE: CONSTITUTIONAL LIMITS ON LAND USE CONTROL AND ENVIRONMENTAL REGULATION (Island Press 1998).

12. Conservation easements protect significant swaths of U.S. land, but their designation and management are increasingly controversial. For a readable introduction into many of the issues, see Richard Conniff, *Why Isn't Publicly Funded Conservation on Private Land More Accountable?* Yale Environment 360 (July 23, 2019), https://e360.yale.edu/features/why-isnt-publicly-funded-conservation-on-private-land-more-accountable.

CHAPTER FOUR

Regulatory Instruments

A regulatory instrument is a set of rules or restrictions that govern an activity, including directions on what happens if people undertake too much, or too little, of that activity. Different types of regulatory instruments work like different tools in a regulator's tool belt. For example, policymakers who wanted to promote energy conservation could use several different tools—regulatory instruments—to accomplish that goal. They might ban energy-hungry industrial activities, or permit new factories to be built only when they are outfitted with energy-efficient technologies; they might tax energy use, or subsidize purchase of energy-efficient home appliances; or they might nudge high-use consumers to reduce their usage by informing them of average use rates. Any of these approaches might successfully further the policy goal of reducing energy use, but each relies on a different instrument to achieve that end.

In principle, legislators have access to the same legal tools and regulatory instruments regardless of the area or type of law in which they are regulating. In practice, the "fit" between the regulatory instrument and the regulatory problem is crucial for its effectiveness. In this regard, the diffuse, complex, and nonhuman character of environmental impacts can pose a real challenge to policymakers; a regulatory instrument that may work very well for fighting crime could prove very ineffective for improving air quality. Similarly, some actors and types of law are better suited to deploying some regulatory instruments.

This chapter sets out the most common types of regulatory instruments and how they are used to address specific environmental problems. It pays particular attention to their strengths and weaknesses in addressing environmental impacts.

HOW DO REGULATORY INSTRUMENTS WORK?

There are many different regulatory instruments, and new ones are continuously being developed and tested, both to deal with new types of activities and to better manage familiar ones.[1] While approaches vary, the common core of all regulatory instruments is that they seek to encourage an actor—typically an individual or a business—to make the "right" decision, or at least to behave as the policymaker prefers. In the context of environmental impacts, the preferred decision may be to do more or less of something (such as to recycle more, to use less water), or to stop doing something entirely (such as to stop activities that harm protected animals). In order to achieve this, regulation provides incentives. These incentives can take multiple forms: they may be financial—for example, taxing an environmentally costly activity; penal—as when someone is imprisoned for creating environmental harm; or sometimes only psychological or behavioral—for example, structuring decisions to make it easier for people to throw away litter, or to behave in other ways that have pro-environmental impacts. Incentives can also be positive or negative—using either "carrots" or "sticks"—by either rewarding "good" behavior or punishing "bad" behavior.

The effectiveness of a specific regulatory instrument—the extent to which the regulation is able to discourage someone from acting in a certain way—depends on many factors, including the type of actor, the type of consequence, and the actor's perceived likelihood that their behavior will be recognized and penalized. The same is true for any positive effect that regulation may create to encourage preferred behaviors.

Social norms can also play an important role vis-à-vis regulatory instruments. Social norms tend to develop through frequent social interactions, not through top-down regulatory processes. As such, they are not a regulatory instrument per se. Nevertheless, their interaction with regulatory instruments is important: people's perception of a law, and their likelihood of compliance, can change depending on whether the law—and the regulatory instrument tasked with enforcing it—is considered consistent with or contrary to social norms.[2] Unjust laws— however defined—are very difficult to enforce, and voluntary compliance with such laws may be limited. Conversely, laws that simply reiterate preexisting social norms need little or even no separate legal enforcement, as the social norms themselves will drive people toward compliance. Indeed, in some cases, social norms alone can be so powerful that communities can effectively regulate resources even in the absence of individual property rights or judicial enforcement.[3]

Importantly, while policymakers generally have particular goals for how they seek to affect behavior—and thus environmental quality— policymakers' assumptions regarding people's motivations and decision making are not always accurate. Sometimes this is because policymakers themselves are subject to psychological and other bias; sometimes it is because policymakers assume that people will behave "rationally," making decisions that optimize their personal well-being. In fact, empirical research increasingly suggests that people face serious psychological and practical constraints in processing and perceiving information, and in translating that information into action. As a result, even when people seek to rationally maximize their self-interest, they frequently struggle to do so. These struggles are heightened where—as in many environmental contexts—people are asked to act in light of environmental impacts, which tend to be distinctively difficult to perceive, understand, and value.[4]

In recent years, regulators in the United States and around the world have begun incorporating insights from psychology and other social sciences into their predictions about how policy instruments are likely to work. One particularly fruitful line of inquiry has led to the development of behavioral instruments, such as nudges, designed to account for and even to leverage people's unconscious cognitive biases. Other social science research is increasingly used to supplement the effectiveness of other regulatory instruments.

TYPES OF INSTRUMENTS

Four types of instruments play a particularly important role in environmental policy: traditional instruments of command-and-control regulation, which work through mandating or banning behaviors; economic instruments, which rely on adjusting prices for behaviors upward or downward; information-based instruments, which rely on disclosure and information provision; and emerging behavioral instruments, such as nudges, which work through purposefully shaping people's decision-making processes.

As a group, *command-and-control regulation* broadly covers all regulation that is founded in the prohibition or prescription of specific behavior, for instance through permits or bans. Command-and-control regulation is easily the most widespread type of regulation, used in various forms in most areas of environmental regulation. Despite its ubiquity, the use of command-and-control regulation is sometimes criticized as inefficient or costly. Furthermore, to prescribe or prohibit behavior, policymakers need a lot of information that the government may not always be in the best place to obtain or interpret.[5] Notably, some behavioral research suggests that bans and other command-and-control regulation may prove more effective when combined with messaging that suggests moral or social disapproval of the regulated action.[6]

Economic instruments do not prohibit or mandate specific behavior. Instead, they provide "prices" on behavior and rely on individuals' private cost-benefit analysis as to whether they wish to continue with their behavior once it becomes costlier. Environmental taxes, for example, do

big biz

not prohibit the use of heavily polluting products, but they make their use less economically viable or appealing. A common way to phrase this is to say that the regulation forces people to "internalize the externalities of their actions." Economic instruments have also been affected by behavioral insights. For example, increased awareness of loss aversion has taught us that a small tax of five cents on disposable bags used at a grocery store is likely to be perceived as a loss from the status quo, whereas a "rebate" of five cents for each reusable bag used is likely to be perceived as a gain. Because people value losses more strongly than equivalent gains, behavioral research suggests that the loss—the tax—is more effective at reducing disposable bag use.[7]

An important application of economic instruments to environmental policy comes with cap-and-trade systems, such as the sulfur dioxide trading scheme implemented under the 1990 amendments to the Clean Air Act. Such schemes create tradable permits that individuals engaged in a certain activity (such as emitting sulfur dioxide) need to purchase to continue their production of environmentally harmful substances. Because allowances tend to be assigned on the basis of historical emissions, lowering emissions through technological progress or less production will result in an excess of emission allowances that can then be sold to others. This means that there is both an absolute *cap* on environmental harm and the potential for economic efficiency in achieving reductions by allowing for *trade*.

Economic instruments are generally considered more cost-effective than command-and-control regulation because they allow the "market" to price the actions that people want to engage in. This means that those with the most information about the regulated behavior can make informed decisions about what is an efficient level of activity, keeping in mind both their private costs and broader public costs (which are theoretically internalized because of the economic instrument). An important limitation of these instruments is that their implementation still relies on good information to get the basic price, or trading scheme, "right." When regulators have poor information, it can undermine economic instruments. For example, in the European Union's Emissions Trading Scheme for greenhouse gases, limited data about historical emissions meant that participants were awarded far more allowances than they needed, which meant there was no economic incentive to reduce emissions.[8] As a result, the economic instrument struggled to work as policymakers had planned. Economic instruments sometimes also meet with moral objections, as some consider the monetization of certain environmental processes to be wrong. For example, when Namibia auctioned a permit to hunt an endangered black rhino for $350,000—with the plan of using the proceeds to protect surviving rhino populations—the decision was met with controversy and protests, as some saw the choice to sell the right to kill an endangered animal as immoral.[9]

Information-based instruments seek to inform people's behavior. Two common forms of information-based instruments are labels and disclosure regimes. Importantly, these instruments do not prescribe a certain type of behavior but rather require people to inform others (or be informed) about the behavior they (or others) engage in. They are often used together with other, possibly more prescriptive, instruments. Examples of this type of regime include organic labeling on food and consumer products, as well as disclosure regimes such as the National Environmental Policy Act (NEPA) and the Emergency Planning and Community Right-to-Know Act (EPCRA). NEPA imposes disclosure requirements on all major governmental actions significantly affecting the environment (see spotlight 11), while EPCRA provides the federal legal regimes for ensuring that people know about dangerous releases of toxic substances.

Building on behavioral research in the social sciences, *behavioral instruments*—tools for regulating behavior that build on empirical research about how people behave—have emerged as a separate category of regulatory instrument over recent years.[10] Several of these instruments build upon the concept of "choice architecture," developed by Nobel Prize–winning economist Richard Thaler and law professor Cass Sunstein, and popularized in their book *Nudge*.[11] The two main

(Paragraph continues on p. 66)

SPOTLIGHT 11. THE NATIONAL ENVIRONMENTAL POLICY ACT

One of the most important environmental laws in the United States, the National Environmental Policy Act (NEPA) plays a pervasive role in how federal actors address the environmental impacts of their actions. It has also been highly influential on the international stage: most countries around the globe have created environmental impact assessment programs modeled on NEPA, making it one of the most replicated statutes in the world.

Passed in 1970, the key instrument in NEPA is information generation and disclosure. NEPA requires agencies to prepare environmental impact statements for major proposed actions that will "significantly affect" "the quality of the human environment."

Environmental impact statements must provide a description of the expected environmental impacts, identify any unavoidable adverse impacts, and identify reasonable alternatives to the proposed action. The statute also requires that agencies provide an opportunity for public review and comment. NEPA is administered by the Council on Environmental Quality, which issues guidance to agencies on how to satisfy the requirements of NEPA.

The Supreme Court has underscored that NEPA is a procedural statute rather than a substantive one: although NEPA requires agencies to analyze and disclose the environmental impacts of their actions, it does not require them to take any particular action in response to that assessment.*

Notably, NEPA lacks any citizen suit provision, which means that citizens cannot sue directly to enforce the terms of the statute. As a result, lawsuits to enforce NEPA requirements are typically brought under the Administrative Procedure Act, and typically allege that the agency in question acted arbitrarily and capriciously by failing to follow NEPA requirements.

Many U.S. states have adopted their own version of NEPA; some of these, such as New York's State Environmental Quality Review

Act (SEQR) and California's California Environmental Quality Act (CEQA), impose substantive as well as procedural requirements on state and local actors. A few, such as Minnesota's Minnesota Environmental Rights Act (MERA), also provide citizen suits that allow "any person" to directly enforce the statute against public actors.

* See *Strycker's Bay Neighborhood Council v. Karlen*, 444 U.S. 223 (1980); *Robertson v. Methow Valley Citizens Council*, 490 U.S. 332 (1989).

applications of choice architecture in the environmental context arise through *default rules* and *framing*.

In regard to default rules, researchers have found, across multiple legal and nonlegal contexts, that they are remarkably "sticky," such that once a rule is identified as the status quo, people have a strong tendency to stick with that rule. Successful environmental applications have included automatically enrolling consumers in green energy programs and/or recycling programs; setting default printer settings to print double-sided instead of single-sided; adopting packaging and sales practices that encourage consumers and businesses to generate less waste, such as providing disposable straws to diners only upon request; and hotel policies to wash linens and towels only upon guest request.[12]

Framing, on the other hand, uses people's reliance on heuristics for quick decision making and the importance of context in our ability to process information. Small changes in how contextual cues are presented or framed can be strategically used to shape people's behaviors. For example, the same option is typically evaluated more favorably when it is seen as the middle or intermediate in the set of options considered, than when it is seen as extreme.[13] Thus, an option for regulatory stringency that is contrasted with two other options—one more stringent and one less stringent—is likely to generate more intuitive support than if the same option were included in a list of all less stringent alternatives. Or consider that framing can be used to associate environmental actions with positive or negative emotions—"smiley" and "frowny" emoticons, for example, have been used effectively to encourage people to use less energy than their neighbors.[14]

Every regulatory instrument has weaknesses as well as strengths (table 3). As a result, the most effective regulatory approach is often not *one* instrument, but a combination of regulatory approaches. For

TABLE 3

Strengths and Weaknesses of Regulatory Instruments

Regulatory Instrument	Strengths	Weaknesses
Command and control • Bans • Permits	• Easy to enforce • Familiar to regulators and society	• Requires a lot of information to be effective • Bans may stop potentially positive innovation
Economic instruments • Taxes • Subsidies • Market-based instruments	• Flexible • Internalizes previously external costs and benefits of activity	• Pricing must be accurate • Moral objections to pricing
Information-based instruments • Labels • Disclosure regimes	• Flexible • Information creation • Possibility for private enforcement • Cheap to implement	• Less coercive • Puts a decision-making burden on private parties
Behavioral instruments • Framing • Default rules	• Builds on preexisting psychological processes • Low enforcement costs	• Can be seen as paternalistic or manipulative • May not account for cultural and social differences

example, using default rules and framing together tends to be more effective than using either one separately: informing homeowners about standard energy use (setting a default usage rate) *and* including an emoticon related to their use (triggering a framing effect) has been found to more effectively reduce energy consumption than just informing people about status quo usage rates.[15] Similarly, using framing alongside command-and-control regulation can improve people's perception of the regulation's requirements, make compliance more likely, and reduce enforcement needs. Finally, policymakers must also consider that the combination of instruments may itself lead to an increase of costs, inefficiencies, or other unintended consequences.

CHOOSING AMONG REGULATORY INSTRUMENTS

Ideally, to regulate most effectively, policymakers would tailor the choice of regulatory instrument to the features of behavior they are regulating. Admittedly, this does not always happen, for a variety of reasons. The policymakers may be unfamiliar with new regulatory techniques—such as behavioral nudges—or may misunderstand the complex environmental problem, or the behavior, they are attempting to regulate. Or they may be focused on protecting industry or private interests, which can be in conflict with public interest, or may be interested only in short-term goals, which can lead to myopic instrument choices. These possibilities suggest the importance of making both policymakers and those who can influence policy aware of the range of instruments that are available for regulating environmental quality. The process of selecting an instrument that presents the best fit between regulatory instrument and problem is generally referred to as *instrument choice*.

Instrument Choice

Scholars and policymakers have invested heavily in the technical skill of instrument choice. This has produced important insights that help policymakers determine the best fit between instrument and regulatory problem. Take, for example, the problem of greenhouse gas emissions, which presents a series of regulatory challenges (as discussed further in chapter 8). In responding to these challenges, policymakers have a number of choices to make about which legal instruments to use to address the problem. They might use command-and-control regulation in the form of an emission standard, which tells specific actors how much they are allowed to emit; an economic mechanism, such as a cap-and-trade scheme or a tax; or a behavioral instrument that attempts to shape behavior by nudging people toward reduced emissions or that merely informs them about how their emissions compare to their neighbors'. All these instruments might lead to a reduction in emissions. But the actual amount of the reduction, and the cost at which it is achieved, varies hugely between the instruments. In order to determine the best fit, therefore, policymakers need to carefully recognize their own goals with respect to the regulatory problem.

Notably, it is almost never the case that policymakers want to put an absolute stop to polluting activities. Rather, environmental law tends to try and balance environmental protection with other societal goals such as economic growth, human health, and scientific development. Instrument choice is thus not only about regulating the activity that leads to the environmental impact, but also about regulating the effects of the regulation itself.

Restrictions on Instrument Choice

Policymakers must manage their instrument choice within a number of institutional, legal, and practical constraints. Institutionally, policymakers are often constrained by the constitutional structure of their government and by their place within it. Most constitutional democracies around the world reserve legislative power—the power to make laws—to elected legislatures. As a result, for either constitutional or political reasons, legislators are often the policymakers who must select the instrument(s) to be used to accomplish legislative goals. In the United States, legislatures typically do this by drafting statutes that identify particular instruments to be used—such as the cap-and-trade regime used to control sulfur dioxide—and then direct an agency to administer that instrument. Depending on how the legislature drafts the statute, the agency may then have great or limited discretion in deciding how the instrument will operate. In the United States, agencies are commonly given substantial discretion of this kind, which allows them to substantially affect how instruments operate on the ground. That said, policymakers at agencies are still legally constrained from choosing instruments that Congress has prohibited.

Other restrictions on instrument choice are practical, such as lack of budget or expertise. These can also influence the choice among regulatory instruments. If a jurisdiction already has an intricate tax system in place, adding another tax will seem relatively low-cost, since no new institutions or even processes for collection would have to be created. The creation of a cap-and-trade system, on the other hand, will almost always present significant start-up costs, including monitoring of previously unmonitored (or undermonitored) activities, setting up a trading space, ensuring the reliability of information on which trades are based, and so on. Many of these restrictions do not technically preclude the choice of an instrument, but they do provide budgetary constraints that may sometimes lead regulators to choose easier or cheaper instruments over more complex or expensive ones. Sometimes, political factors may play a role in these practicalities: for instance, cutting an agency's budget will affect its ability to monitor certain activities and/or adopt certain regulatory instruments. It is therefore important to consider the laws that shape instrument choice—and the actors empowered to adopt such laws—alongside the specific strengths and weaknesses of specific regulatory instruments.

Finally, policymakers are sometimes limited by cognitive and historical processes that make it difficult for them to shift away from past instrument choices. Most environmental regulation in force today is command-and-control regulation, which as we have noted can be criticized as being costly (for the regulator and regulated), inflexible, and dependent on only partially available information. Why, then, is it still so pervasive? One of the answers to this question is *path dependency*, which causes people to continue existing practices even when better ones could be adopted. Path dependency is caused mainly by the transaction costs that such a shift from existing to new practices would entail. A real-life example is the continued use of the QWERTY keyboard, despite the fact that it has long been proven that another ordering of keys would lead to more efficient and faster typing. However, the costs of having to replace all existing keyboards and retrain all current typists to a new keyboard weighs more heavily than any potential efficiency gains.

In some situations, path dependency is a logical outcome of a cost-benefit analysis. But in many situations, the form that existing legislation has taken will determine the shape of future legislation and regulatory instruments regardless of the cost-benefit analysis of change. The basic command-and-control framework of the Clean Air Act of 1970 has remained substantially the same through every subsequent major amendment, including those in 1974, 1977, and 1990, despite the addition of new programs and some changes to preexisting parts of the statute. This is also true for the U.S. Clean Water Act and other pollution-control statutes, none of which have been meaningfully changed for nearly a half-century.[16] The historical developments that lead to the adoption of one instrument can thus also influence many future instrument choices through path dependency.

Apart from high transition costs, the adoption of new instruments, or the change of existing ones, also presents *compliance costs* to the actors affected by the regulatory instrument. Furthermore, policymakers may sometimes be subject to political pressure and influence, which can affect the substance of their decisions. Often the simple act of gathering the necessary information for instrument design and implementation requires exchanges with industry representatives and environmental NGOs, both of which may try to influence the regulatory process through the informational advantages they have vis-à-vis the policy-maker. Such regulatory capture can lead to less or more stringent environmental regulation. Counterintuitively, it is not always the case that an economically powerful firm engaged in environmentally damaging behavior will push for *less* stringent regulation; more stringent and costly regulation can create a competitive advantage against smaller firms, or even a barrier to entry to the market, which would be in the larger firm's interest. Budget restraints and/or lack of expertise on the side of the policymaker make regulatory capture more likely, which in turn can have an important impact on instrument choice and design.

SUMMARY

Environmental law sets out societal goals with respect to the management of environmental impacts. In order to incentivize individuals, companies, and other actors involved in environmentally impactful activities, policymakers are tasked with designing regulatory instruments. These instruments harness financial, penal, psychological, and social motivations in order to change behaviors.

The choice among regulatory instruments—which include command-and-control regulation, economic instruments, information-based instruments, and behavioral instruments—would ideally prioritize the fit between environmental impact and regulatory instrument. Proper fit is most likely to produce changes in the behavior leading to environmental impacts. However, there are important constraints on instrument choice, such as legal and practical restrictions as to the available tools, as well as historical and cognitive processes that restrain policymakers' ability to choose freely among instruments.

TAKEAWAYS

✓ Regulatory instruments are used to incentivize individuals, companies, and other actors to act to further environmental goals.

✓ Commonly used instruments include command-and-control instruments, economic instruments, information-based instruments, and behavioral instruments.

✓ Instrument choice is aimed at choosing the "best" instrument to achieve certain types of behavior. What the best choice is depends on one's view of the relative pros and cons of various factors, including the importance of cost of regulation, cost of enforcement, cost of compliance, and stringency of goals.

✓ Instrument choice can also be constrained by legal, institutional, historical, or practical concerns regarding the power of the regulator and the rights of the party that is being regulated.

KEY TERMS

BEHAVIORAL INSTRUMENTS Instruments for regulating behavior that build on social science research, particularly in psychology and behavioral economics.

CAP-AND-TRADE SYSTEM A regulatory instrument that sets a maximum cap on a certain activity (e.g., emitting activities) and allows participants to trade permits with each other to engage in more or less of that activity.

CHOICE ARCHITECTURE Purposeful structuring of decision-making contexts to shape people's behavior toward selected ends.

COMMAND-AND-CONTROL REGULATION A group of regulatory instruments that rely on standard setting in order to permit or ban certain types of behavior.

COMPLIANCE COSTS The cost of complying with a regulatory standard.

DEFAULT RULES A preset course of action that takes effect automatically, unless decision makers provide an alternative specification.

ECONOMIC INSTRUMENTS Regulatory instruments that rely on economic incentives in order to achieve compliance.

EXTERNALITIES Costs or benefits created by an activity that are experienced by parties other than the one engaged in the activity.

FRAMING A behavioral instrument that uses small changes in how contextual cues are presented to strategically shape people's behaviors.

INSTRUMENT CHOICE Selection among different types of regulatory instruments with a view to create the "best" fit between the regulated behavior and the method of regulation.

MARKET-BASED REGULATION A regulation that makes use of economic incentives created by markets.

NUDGE A behavioral instrument that is meant to alter people's behavior in predictable ways, without forbidding any options or significantly changing economic incentives.

PATH DEPENDENCY A phenomenon whereby people continue existing practices even where better ones could be adopted, because of the costs associated with shifting to new "paths" or practices.

REGULATORY INSTRUMENT A tool that a policymaker uses to achieve regulatory goals.

DISCUSSION QUESTIONS

1. Should the choice about regulatory instruments be made by legislators or agencies? On what basis?

2. Do economically powerful firms always want less environmental regulation? When might they push for more regulation?

3. How much should cost considerations (compliance and/or enforcement costs) weigh in the choice of instrument?

4. What are the best ways to ensure flexibility in regulatory instruments? What kind of flexibility is most important in addressing environmental impacts? Link your answer to specific examples.

5. If people do not realize that they are being "regulated" (for instance, through the use of default rules or framing), is this desirable, or problematic? Why?

6. A regulatory instrument that was not discussed in this chapter is voluntary self-regulation, whereby companies or industries create rules for themselves. What might be the advantages and disadvantages of such regulation with respect to environmental impacts?

7. How important do you think it is that something is considered morally wrong as well as legally wrong, especially with respect to the regulation of environmental impacts? Give an example from your personal experience.

NOTES

1. See Policy Instruments in Environmental Law (Kenneth Richards and Josephine van Zeben eds., Edward Elgar 2020).

2. See Janice Nadler, *Flouting the Law*, 83 Texas L. Rev. 1399 (2005).

3. Elinor Ostrom, Governing the Commons (Cambridge University Press 1990).

4. See Arden Rowell and Kenworthey Bilz, The Psychology of Environmental Law (NYU Press 2021).

5. As discussed in more detail below.

6. See Kenworthey Bilz and Janice Nadler, *Law Psychology, and Morality*, in Psychology of Learning and Motivation (Elsevier 2009).

7. Related research suggests that imposing a small tax rather than a ban may also prove more effective, again because of the psychological effects of loss aversion. For a readable summary of several U.S. cities' experience with plastic bag bans and taxes, see Antonio Perez, "How Behavioral Science Solved Chicago's Plastic Bag Problem," Politico.com (November 21, 2019).

8. See Josephine van Zeben, The Allocation of Regulatory Competence in the European Emissions Trading System (Cambridge University Press 2014).

9. See Jon Herskovitz, *Permit to Hunt Endangered Rhinoceros Sells for $350,000 Despite Protests*, Reuters, Jan. 11, 2014, www.reuters.com/article/us-usa-rhino-auction-idUSBREA0B02720140112.

10. Arden Rowell, *Behavioural Instruments in Environmental Regulation,* in POLICY INSTRUMENTS IN ENVIRONMENTAL LAW (Kenneth Richards and Josephine van Zeben eds., Edward Elgar 2020).

11. See Richard Thaler and Cass Sunstein, NUDGE (Yale University Press 2008); see also Thaler and Sunstein, *Libertarian Paternalism Is Not an Oxymoron,* 70 U. CHI. L. REV. 1159 (2003).

12. See Hilary Byerly et al., *Nudging Pro-environmental Behavior: Evidence and Opportunities,* 16 FRONTIERS ECOLOGY & ENV'T 159 (2017); see also Cass Sunstein and Lucia Reisch, *Automatically Green: Behavioral Economics and Environmental Regulation,* 38 HARV. ENVTL. L. REV. 127–158 (2013).

13. See Mark Kelman et al., *Context-Dependence in Legal Decision Making,* 25 J. LEGAL STUD. 287 (1996). This phenomenon is sometimes called the "compromise effect."

14. See Wesley Shultz et al., *The Constructive, Destructive, and Reconstructive Power of Social Norms,* 18 PSYCHOL. SCI. 429 (2007); see also Elisha Frederiks, Karen Stenner, and Elizabeth Hobman, *Household Energy Use: Applying Behavioral Economics to Understand Consumer Decision-Making and Behavior,* 41 RENEWABLE & SUSTAINABLE ENERGY REVIEWS 1385 (2015).

15. See Shultz et al., *supra* note 9.

16. Daniel Cole, *Explaining the Persistence of "Command-and-Control" in US Environmental Law, in* POLICY INSTRUMENTS IN ENVIRONMENTAL LAW (Kenneth Richards and Josephine van Zeben eds., Edward Elgar, 2020).

PART TWO

U.S. Environmental Law

CHAPTER FIVE

Contextualizing
U.S. Environmental Law

This chapter highlights three key features of the U.S. legal system that—although most were not developed specifically to deal with environmental impacts—nevertheless respond to, and interact with, the challenges created by those impacts. To contextualize these features, the chapter starts with a short introduction to the history of U.S. environmental regulation. It then expands on the role of federalism, the role of regulatory agencies, and the concepts of risk analysis and cost-benefit analysis in U.S. environmental law.

Readers who are already familiar with the U.S. legal system may choose to begin the book here. Readers who are new to the U.S. legal system will find it helpful to first review the materials included in part I of this volume.

A BRIEF HISTORY OF U.S. ENVIRONMENTAL REGULATION

The earliest U.S. environmental laws had their roots in state common law doctrines, such as the doctrine of nuisance. In the late nineteenth and early twentieth centuries, the conservation movement—often associated with President Theodore Roosevelt—helped establish several of the nation's most important federal land management systems and agencies, including the National Forest System in 1891 and the National Park Service in 1916. In addition, a few early federal statutes, most notably the Migratory Bird Treaty Act of 1918, implemented international environmental treaties.

Modern U.S. environmental law, however, is generally traced to the environmental movement that began in the 1960s. (See time line in appendix.) In 1962, biologist Rachel Carson's extraordinarily influential book *Silent Spring* was published, jump-starting the environmental movement and highlighting the environmental impacts of toxic substances. A series of environmental disasters throughout the 1960s—including the Cuyahoga River in Ohio catching on fire, and the Santa Barbara oil spill of 1969 blanketing the waters of the Santa Barbara channel in oil—raised environmental consciousness still further.

On January 1, 1970, President Richard Nixon signed the National Environmental Policy Act into law, launching what is sometimes known as the "Environmental Decade" in U.S. environmental law. The same year saw the establishment of the Environmental Protection Agency (EPA). The next ten years saw remarkably speedy—and largely uncontroversial—passage of many of the major federal environmental statutes still in place today, including the Clean Air Act (1970); the Occupational Safety and Health Act (1970); the Federal Insecticide, Fungicide, and Rodenticide Act (1972); the Clean Water Act (1972); the Endangered Species Act (1973); the Safe Drinking Water Act (1974); the Resource Conservation and Recovery Act (1976); the Toxic Substances Control Act (1976); the Comprehensive Environmental Response, Compensation, and Liability Act (or "Superfund," 1980); and a number of important amendments. In most cases, these statutes delegated significant authority to administrative agencies, and particularly to the EPA.

Although the pace of new legislation slowed during the 1980s under the overtly deregulatory presidency of Ronald Reagan, other important environmental mechanisms were developed during that time. In particular, the 1980s saw the creation—and entrenchment—of new forms of regulatory analysis, as well as the participation of the United States in the influential Montreal Protocol on Substances that Deplete the Ozone Layer (1987). The 1990s saw the substantive amendment of the Clean Air Act, and substantial debate regarding U.S. participation in international climate change agreements—particularly the Kyoto Protocol, which the United States ultimately chose not to ratify. During the 2000s and 2010s, the relative scarcity of new federal legislation on environmental matters—including climate change—left many substantive environmental policy decisions in the hands of environmental agencies, and of the President. At times, as between the presidencies of Barack Obama (2009–17) and Donald Trump (2017–), this has led to substantial shifts in federal environmental policy between presidential administrations.

THREE DISTINCTIVE FEATURES
OF U.S. ENVIRONMENTAL LAW

To understand how modern U.S. environmental law functions, it is important to understand several distinctive features of the U.S. approach: namely, federalism; the role of regulatory agencies; and the concepts of risk analysis and cost-benefit analysis. These features give U.S. environmental law its unique flavor and present one of many potential formulas for managing the puzzling question of how humans should shape the world in which they live.

The Role of Federalism

The United States relies on a governmental system of federalism, a structure of government that unites separate regional governments (in the United States, the states) with a general government (in the United States, the federal or U.S. government) to create a single political system. This structure relies on overlapping areas of geographic and subject-matter jurisdiction, or legal authority, while allowing states to remain independent for some purposes. In principle, this allows issues to be resolved at local levels when they are best resolved locally, at federal levels when they are best handled nationally, and at state levels when they are best managed at an intermediate stage of geographic concentration.

The existence of multiple levels of governance allows for variance across the fifty states that make up the United States. This presents at least two benefits: it creates a "laboratory of states" that can experiment with different solutions to challenging problems; and it allows for a variety of resolutions to controversial environmental issues, so that people with differing beliefs and preferences are more likely to be able to find a place of residence that fits their preferred way of life. To leverage these features, sometimes the federal government and state governments work together in a model called *cooperative federalism*, where the federal government works as a coordinator, and individual states are responsible for managing impacts that fall within their geographic area of concern. The primary law governing air pollution in the United States—the Clean Air Act—relies heavily on this structure.

For environmental purposes, a key drawback of federalism is that political boundaries do not always match the geographic distribution of environmental impacts. For example, water pollution tends to be a much more localized issue than air pollution, and the geographic range of either form of pollution may have little relation to state borders. U.S. federalism also provides limited guidance for the management of internationally dispersed environmental impacts beyond the borders of the United States, which presents challenges for managing global and international environmental issues like climate change. Moreover, while federalism accommodates variance among states, it also increases legal complexity and can create problems of coordination between (state) governments. This is particularly problematic when the political boundaries of the states are a poor fit for the geographic dispersal of a particular environmental impact—for example, in the management of water rights from rivers that run through multiple states. The latter example arises particularly often in the relatively arid western United States, where water resources are limited and must be shared, and regulated, by several states. In some cases, the United States manages this challenge by allocating coordinating authority to the federal government, as in the Clean Air Act example above. In others, as with water rights in the West, the resulting scheme comprises a confused patchwork of conflicting claims and competing state laws.

The Role of Administrative Agencies

A second distinctive aspect of U.S. law, even within the federalist system, is the centrality of administrative agencies in addressing many issues, including many environmental problems. As was discussed in chapter 2, administrative agencies are units of government created by statute to build and leverage a reservoir of expertise.[1] Federal statutes frequently empower agencies to make prospective regulations, to enforce those regulations, and even to adjudicate cases within their areas of expertise. The sheer size and scope of the U.S. *regulatory state*— the term sometimes used to refer to the entire network of hundreds of U.S. administrative agencies, and the critical government functions they perform—sometimes comes as a surprise even to many Americans. In addition to employing more than two million Americans, and to setting and enforcing rules with compliance costs over $1 trillion a year, modern agencies also create more binding rules of conduct than Congress, and adjudicate more cases than federal courts.

Many commentators consider the 1930s, and the presidency of Franklin D. Roosevelt, to mark the birth of the modern regulatory state. For environmental purposes, however, the creation of the EPA in 1970 is at least as important a benchmark. Throughout the Environmental Decade and beyond, the EPA and other agencies were delegated more and more authority, via a series of environmental statutes, including those addressing air pollution, water pollution, toxic substances, and contaminated sites.[2] As a result, environmental agencies became a more and more important actor in U.S. environmental law.

One underappreciated consequence of the rise of the regulatory state is that empowering agencies also tends to empower the executive branch. Generally speaking, environmental agencies are so-called "executive" agencies, which means that they fall under the direction of the President. For executive agencies, the President has the authority to choose (with the consent of the Senate) whom to appoint as the head of an agency, and the President can unilaterally fire the head of the agency at any time, for any reason, including political reasons. This and other executive powers give Presidents significant control over what agencies choose to prioritize, and how they choose to implement the statutes they administer. That said, while executive control of agency personnel is a powerful tool for Presidents to direct regulatory policy, it is also possible to overestimate how much power Presidents hold over agencies. The other branches of government also have mechanisms for constraining (or empowering) agencies—Congress through lawmaking and through writing the statutes that agencies administer, and the judiciary through the power of judicial review. Furthermore, while the principal officers in agencies are appointed by the President, the vast majority of U.S. agency employees are in fact career civil servants, who acquire their jobs through competitive, merit-based procedures, and are protected from firing absent unusual circumstances. Most scientists, economists, and technical experts within agencies, therefore, will keep their jobs through multiple presidential administrations.

The role of regulatory agencies in U.S. law remains somewhat politically controversial. Because agency employees are never directly elected by voters, some critics of the regulatory state worry that the extent of authority wielded by regulatory agencies is undemocratic. On the flipside, defenders of the regulatory state often point to the social advantages of having agency decisions driven by expertise, rather than being set entirely by reference to political will.

The Role of Risk Analysis and Cost-Benefit Analysis

Because administrative agencies set significant amounts of U.S. environmental policy, it is important to understand the decision-making procedures they use to decide how to address environmental problems. Two aspects of agency decision making that influence environmental law are risk analysis and cost-benefit analysis.

Risk analysis—a systemized method for identifying, assessing, quantifying, and evaluating risks—was initially developed within administrative agencies, for which it continues to be a key tool. Traditionally, U.S. risk analysis has attempted to separate the political and scientific aspects of risk analysis by splitting it into two stages: risk assessment and risk management. Risk assessment involves assessing and quantifying the probabilities and magnitudes of hazards associated with particular behaviors and policies.[3] It involves asking and answering questions like these: What type of risk does a pollutant pose to human health or the environment? What is the magnitude of that risk, how likely is it, and in what quantities can the ill effect be expected? Risk management, by contrast, involves policy-based decisions about which and how risks will be reduced or tolerated.[4] It involves asking and answering questions like these: How much of the pollutant should be tolerated, in light of the harms it can be expected to cause and the reasons it is being emitted? What quantity of that pollutant (if any) should a particular industry or company be permitted to emit?

The use of risk analysis by administrative agencies helps address the technical and complex nature of environmental impacts by pooling expertise, and by creating a systematic approach to collecting, assessing, and implementing scientific information. Although courts maintain a role in reviewing agency risk analyses, they tend to defer to the technical expertise of agencies in the types of factual matters that make environmental impacts so complex.

A key feature of risk analysis as a building block of the U.S. approach to environmental law is that it explicitly links scientific research and environmental policy. The systemization of this relationship tends to increase the transparency of environmental decision making, rendering it more susceptible to review by courts, the public, and the other branches of government. The quantification of risk that is central to risk analysis also provides valuable benchmarks for comparing the diverse environmental impacts that can attach to individual human behaviors.

That said, the formalist separation between science and policy on which risk analysis is based is sometimes hard to maintain,[5] and some critics believe that continued attempts to segregate scientific and political processes can obscure areas of politicized science.[6] Risk analysis also struggles to handle uncertainty and limited information: where there is no information about the probability of a risk coming to fruition, or of the type or magnitude of the harm if it does, risk analysis provides very limited guidance for policymakers.[7] While risk analysis is aimed at managing the complexity of environmental impacts, unquantifiable or uncertain risks also pose particular challenges for the use of risk analysis in contexts like climate change or the development of new chemical substances.[8]

A second critical concept to understand in regard to internal agency decision making is the role of regulatory cost-benefit analysis (see spotlight 12). Cost-benefit analysis, as practiced in the United States, is a method of quantifying the impacts of a proposed policy, by monetizing all of its negative and positive expected impacts. The theory behind this practice is that it converts diverse impacts—financial costs, mortality risks, loss of ecosystem services—into the single metric of money, thus facilitating comparison of dissimilar impacts to one another.[9]

A key advantage of cost-benefit analysis is that it allows U.S. policymakers to compare diverse types and magnitudes of impact. This includes comparisons of impacts that are diffuse through time: cost-benefit analysis incorporates the process of "discounting," which makes monetary amounts comparable to one another regardless of when those amounts accrue. The systemized nature of the process also helps in comparing policies that have significant immediate costs but long-term delayed benefits—for example, when an agency is deciding whether or not to require a factory to install a costly technology that will reduce

(Paragraph continues on p. 88)

SPOTLIGHT 12. EXECUTIVE ORDERS AND COST-BENEFIT ANALYSIS

Since the 1980s, U.S. agencies have operated under a series of executive orders requiring them to perform a cost-benefit analysis prior to issuing major regulations, including major environmental regulations. These analyses are reviewed by a centralized office in the executive branch called the Office of Information and Regulatory Affairs (OIRA), which is part of the Office of Management and Budget. To pass review by OIRA, agencies must show "a reasoned determination that the benefits of the intended regulation justify its costs." This centralized review invests significant power in the Administrator of OIRA, who, as a result, is known colloquially as the U.S. "regulatory czar."

The general requirement to perform cost-benefit analyses prior to promulgating major regulations has importantly shaped the way in which U.S. agencies manage environmental (and other) issues. As a result of this policy, environmental economics research plays a particularly important role within U.S. environmental agencies, which rely on their economists to help identify ways to monetize the environmental impacts of proposed regulations.

Although most major regulations are subject to the executive requirement to perform cost-benefit analyses, the reach of all executive orders is limited by the constitutional power of the President, and "to the extent permitted by law." This means that the general executive requirements on cost-benefit analysis do not apply when a statute unambiguously prohibits an agency from considering cost, or from incorporating a cost-benefit analysis into its decision making. A few important environmental regimes—most notably the National Ambient Air Quality Standards under the Clean Air Act—do unambiguously bar agencies from considering cost.* But most environmental statutes either explicitly permit consideration of cost or

---

* See *Whitman v. American Trucking*, 531 U.S. 457 (2001).

are silent or ambiguous about the use of cost-benefit analysis. In such cases, the Supreme Court has held that agencies have "discretion" to choose whether to rely on cost-benefit analyses or not.** As a practical matter, while this leaves the agency unbound by congressional dictate, the agency is still bound by the direction of the executive. As a result, most major U.S. environmental regulations are prepared with cost-benefit analyses.

** See *Entergy Corp. v. Riverkeeper,* 556 U.S. 208 (2009).

pollution emissions over subsequent decades. Because risk analysis and cost-benefit analysis are so central to agency decision making, agencies like the EPA invest significant resources in building institutional expertise regarding the quantification and monetization of environmental impacts. For example, the EPA has invested in developing a way to quantify and monetize the types of "ecosystem services" provided by wetlands and other land uses, and it maintains a permanent office of PhD-educated economists at the National Center of Environmental Economics to help advise on quantifying and monetizing environmental impacts.

Despite its central role within U.S. environmental decision making, cost-benefit analysis remains controversial. Much of this controversy revolves around the aspect of cost-benefit analysis that also forms much of its appeal: its dependence on quantification and monetization. While these processes allow for cross-comparison, they can also introduce inaccuracies and omissions. These inaccuracies and omissions can be particularly problematic in environmental contexts, in which many of the impacts are hard to monetize because they are not typically bought and sold. Relatedly, while the process of discounting allows for comparisons of monetized impacts through time, the implementation of discounting remains highly debated. Some critics also worry that the process of cost-benefit analysis can commodify nonmonetary values in worrisome ways (can we put a price on fresh air or biodiversity?), and that the approach is insensitive to the distribution of harms and benefits across a population. Finally, cost-benefit analysis tends to be highly anthropocentric: while it is routinely used to assess the value people attach to nonhuman environmental impacts, it is centrally concerned with the costs and benefits of various policies to humans, not to the environment itself.

SUMMARY

After providing a brief history of the development of environmental law in the United States, this chapter set out several important themes that underlie the U.S. approach to environmental law: federalism, the central role of administrative agencies, and the administrative approaches of risk analysis and cost-benefit analysis. These themes inform U.S. treatment of environmental problems, including pollution, ecosystem degradation, and climate change.

TAKEAWAYS

✓ Modern U.S. environmental law is often traced to the Environmental Decade of the 1970s.

✓ The U.S. approach to environmental law is distinctive for its reliance on federalism, the central role of administrative agencies, and risk analysis and cost-benefit analysis.

KEY TERMS

AGENCIES Units of government created by statute.

COMMON LAW Law made by judges, published in the form of judicial opinions, which gives precedential authority to prior court decisions (may be public or private law).

COOPERATIVE FEDERALISM System of cooperation between federal and state governments, commonly used in the implementation of U.S. pollution control statutes.

COST-BENEFIT ANALYSIS A decision procedure for quantifying (and typically monetizing) the expected positive and negative impacts of a proposed policy.

DISCOUNTING The process of making future (monetary) amounts comparable to current amounts.

ENVIRONMENT The surroundings or conditions in which humans, plants, and animals function.

ENVIRONMENTAL IMPACTS Consequences (generally of human actions) for the surroundings or conditions in which humans, plants, and animals function.

ENVIRONMENTAL JUSTICE Fair distribution of environmental impacts.

ENVIRONMENTAL LAW The use of law to regulate human behaviors with environmental impacts.

FEDERALISM System (and principle) of government in which several states form a union for some purposes while remaining independent for others.

JUDICIAL Of, or relating to, courts or judges.

JURISDICTION The authority to make legally binding decisions within a given territory or subject area.

REGULATIONS Binding rules of legal conduct issued by agencies; may also refer to the action or process, by any legal actor, of limiting or encouraging patterns of behavior.

RISK ANALYSIS A systemized method for identifying, assessing, quantifying, and evaluating risks.

RISK ASSESSMENT The scientific and technical first "stage" of risk analysis where the probabilities and magnitudes of hazards associated with particular behaviors and policies are identified and quantified.

RISK MANAGEMENT The second "stage" of risk analysis, in which policy-based decisions are made about which and how risks will be reduced or tolerated.

DISCUSSION QUESTIONS

1. Many of the most important U.S. environmental statutes trace to the "Environmental Decade" of the 1970s. What advantages or disadvantages do you see in regulating environmental problems on the basis of legal schemes established half a century ago?

2. What might explain the explosion of U.S. environmental laws in the 1970s, and what might explain the relative scarcity of new federal environmental schemes since?

3. How should society balance the values of democratic government and the importance of informing environmental policy with high-quality information and science? Is it more important for environmental law to reflect the best science and the judgment of technical experts, or to reflect the values of the human population who must live under the environmental laws?

4. Is it appropriate to "monetize" environmental quality? Why or why not? If environmental quality is not monetized, what is the best way to decide how much money should be spent on environmental quality? What should we do if people attach different monetary values to environmental quality?

5. Which U.S. legal strategies in environmental law could be used most effectively by other jurisdictions? Which would be difficult to imitate? Why?

NOTES

1. The powers of the U.S. legislature, executive, and judiciary are established—and limited—by the U.S. Constitution, not by statute. See chapter 2 for a discussion of the key actors in U.S. environmental law.

2. See chapter 2 for further discussion of environmental agencies.

3. EPA maintains a number of resources for environmental risk assessment on its website at www.epa.gov/risk/risk-assessment-guidelines. The resources

include EPA's own technical guidelines, as well as a series of readable "citizen guides" on environmental risk assessment topics like air pollution and health risk.

4. EPA describes its general risk management policy at www.epa.gov/risk /risk-management, though in fact the priorities of policymakers at executive agencies like EPA tend to shift with presidential administrations.

5. The bifurcated approach to risk assessment and risk management was embedded in U.S. agency practice in 1983, with the National Academy of Sciences handbook *Risk Assessment in the Federal Government: Managing the Process*, and remains highly influential to this day. That said, more recent guidance from the National Academy of Sciences has itself criticized an overly bifurcated process and recommends further integration of the two. See National Research Council, SCIENCE AND DECISIONS: ADVANCING RISK ASSESSMENT (National Academies Press 2008).

6. A significant literature has grown up around the idea that some risk issues are "trans-scientific," in that they can be posed to science but not resolved by science alone. See Alvin Weinberg, *Science and Trans-Science*, 10 MINERVA 209 (1972). See also, e.g., Wendy Wagner, *The Science Charade in Toxic Risk Regulation*, 95 COLUM. L. REV. 1613 (1995). One important concern in this literature is that trans-scientific issues may be exploited for political purposes.

7. For a helpful discussion of characterizations of risk and uncertainty, particularly as they apply to environmental legal contexts, see Dan Farber, *Uncertainty*, 99 GEO. L.J. 901 (2010).

8. For a discussion of the limits of quantification, see Cass Sunstein, *The Limits of Quantification*, 102 CAL. L. REV. 1369 (2014); Richard Revesz, *Quantifying Regulatory Benefits*, 102 CAL. L. REV. 1423 (2014).

9. The monetization process is typically done by reference to the amount of money people would be willing to pay to reduce those impacts. Sometimes this "willingness to pay" is measured by surveys, and other times it is measured by looking at people's actual economic choices (such as whether to take a riskier or a safer job, or to buy a riskier or a safer product). For a thoughtful discussion of cost-benefit analysis in practice and theory, see Michael A. Livermore and Richard L. Revesz, REVIVING RATIONALITY: SAVING COST-BENEFIT ANALYSIS FOR THE SAKE OF THE ENVIRONMENT AND OUR HEALTH (Oxford University Press 2020).

CHAPTER SIX

Pollution Control

This chapter provides a primer on the U.S. legal approach to pollution control. It begins by defining the general problem of pollution. It then describes the fundamentals of the U.S. approach to controlling pollution, before providing snapshots of individual legal strategies used for particular types of pollution: air pollution, water pollution, soil pollution, toxic substances, and waste.

POLLUTION AS AN ENVIRONMENTAL PROBLEM

Pollution is the presence of higher-than-normal concentrations of unwanted materials (often in the air, water, or soil) that may have adverse effects on humans or on nonhuman organisms.

Pollution control laws aim to (1) control human activities that lead to pollution and (2) limit the harms caused by pollution. These goals are often pursued through two general strategies: *source reduction* and *exposure reduction*. Source reduction involves reducing the amount of pollution created in the first place (at the "source")—for example, by requiring industry to adopt technologies that generate less waste or by encouraging consumers to recycle. Exposure reduction involves amending behaviors so that there is less exposure to pollution—for example, by encouraging people to evacuate after a toxic waste spill or by identifying products that contain dangerous substances.

Pollution can occur when unwanted materials are deposited in the air, water, or soil. Some of these materials, such as many chemicals and toxic substances, are purposefully created because they offer benefits as well as potential dangers. Other substances, such as hazardous waste, are without intrinsic value, and are created only as waste byproducts of daily life or of industrial processes. Each type of pollution—air pollution, water pollution, soil pollution, toxic substances, and waste—presents its own challenges and opportunities for regulation, often related to the specific characteristics of the medium of pollution. Air pollution, for example, tends to be far more mobile—and thus far more likely to create diffuse and distant impacts—than soil pollution, the impact of which tends to be relatively local.

Although each medium of pollution has its own characteristics, pollution control regimes also face common challenges, which can be traced back to the diffuse, complex, and nonhuman nature of environmental impacts. In particular, polluting activity is often far in space and time both from the exposures to pollution and from the harm those exposures cause. Tracing the causal relationships between pollution emission and harm is therefore often difficult. Furthermore, the same pollutant can create different impacts depending on its concentration, the form of exposure, and even its location. Scientists attempt to track the relationship between the amount of pollution exposure (the "dose") and the harm (the "response") it causes through what are called dose-response relationships; understanding such relationships is research intensive, however, and can be highly uncertain, particularly at low levels of exposure. The location of a pollutant can also matter. An interesting example of this is ozone, which poses significant risks to human health when found at the ambient or ground level, but which shields against ultraviolet radiation at the atmospheric level, protecting humans from sunburn and skin cancer. Furthermore, pollution affects nonhuman animals, plants, and ecosystems as well as human populations. At atmospheric levels, for example, ozone protects humans, but it also reduces plankton growth in the oceans, leading to diminished fish stocks and stunted plant growth. The complexity of pollution impacts thus necessitates a strong connection between pollution control policy and scientific research.

An additional challenging aspect of pollution control comes from the interaction between pollution types and media. To effectively control pollution, policymakers must consider how pollution control regimes interact with one another, as well as with other regulatory and legal requirements. One important aspect of this challenge is cross-media pollution, which arises when pollutants are transferred from one environmental medium (such as air) to another (such as water): waste practices that allow for incineration may affect air pollution, for example, and contaminated water may end up depositing pollution into soil. As a result, policymakers must consider not only the best stringency for particular pollution control regimes, but also how those regimes may impact other polluting behaviors.

Finally, competing normative and political values also create challenges for pollution control, as different people and different institutional actors often differ on how much pollution is tolerable, how clean is clean enough, how to balance nonhuman and human interests, and whether the distribution of harms (and profit) from pollution is fair.

KEY CHARACTERISTICS OF POLLUTION CONTROL IN THE UNITED STATES

Every year, the United States of America produces millions of tons of pollution and spends tens of billions of dollars controlling that pollution. The U.S. approach to controlling this pollution is characterized by a complex interweaving of multiple legal actors and tools.

Early pollution control in the United States was mostly managed through the judicial system, through the common law tort of nuisance. Polluters were sued in court after they polluted and were sometimes required to pay damages and/or to cease their pollution[1]—provided that the plaintiffs could meet the (often overwhelming) burden of

TABLE 4

Key U.S. Pollution Control Statutes

Type	Statutes
General	• Pollution Prevention Act (PPA)
Air	• Clean Air Act (CAA)
Water	• Clean Water Act (CWA) • Safe Drinking Water Act (SDWA)
Soil	• Comprehensive Environmental Response, Compensation, and Liability Act (CERCLA) • Surface Mining Control and Reclamation Act (SMCRA) • Marine Protection, Research and Sanctuaries Act (MPRSA) ("Ocean Dumping Act")
Toxic Substances	• Toxic Substances Control Act (TSCA) • Federal Insecticide, Fungicide, and Rodenticide Act (FIFRA) • Emergency Planning and Community Right-to-know Act (EPCRA)
Waste Management	• Resource Conservation and Recovery Act (RCRA) • Comprehensive Environmental Response, Compensation, and Liability Act (CERCLA) • Nuclear Waste Policy Act (NWPA)

showing that the polluting activity had caused them harm. Common law remained the primary source of laws on U.S. pollution control until the 1970s, when the "Environmental Decade" saw the passage of most of the United States' key pollution control statutes (table 4), including the Clean Air Act and the Clean Water Act, and the creation of the Environmental Protection Agency (EPA).

Through the years, Congress has given significant authority to the EPA to administer federal pollution control statutes. At the same time, many of the key pollution control statutes adopt a structure of cooperative federalism, intended to allow the federal government to work cooperatively with states by allowing states to decide how to implement requirements. The federal government's role is to provide minimal standards, oversight, and—if necessary—the capacity to regulate where states have failed to meet standards. In part because states and local governments usually retain significant authority in deciding how to implement pollution control requirements, many states have also developed their own state environmental agencies.

The federal Pollution Prevention Act of 1990 provides a formal statement of the U.S. approach to pollution control (see spotlight 13). The Act formally recognizes the problem of pollution in the United States and adopts a hierarchy of preferred approaches to pollution control. In particular, it encourages potential polluters to invest in cost-effective technologies for reducing pollution, and to prefer reduced creation of pollutants "whenever feasible."

WHO CONTROLS POLLUTION IN THE UNITED STATES?

Pollution control in the United States is a shared effort among actors from all branches of government at both the federal and state levels. To better understand the powers, responsibilities, and strengths of these actors, this section first outlines federal and state roles in pollution control and the consequences of this division of labor, before discussing the parts played by the different branches of government.

SPOTLIGHT 13. POLLUTION PREVENTION ACT OF 1990

National U.S. policy formalizes the following goals in the Pollution Prevention Act of 1990:

- Pollution should be prevented or reduced at the source whenever feasible.
- Pollution that cannot be prevented should be recycled in an environmentally safe manner whenever feasible.
- Pollution that cannot be prevented or recycled should be treated in an environmentally safe manner whenever feasible.
- Disposal or other release into the environment should be employed only as a last resort and should be conducted in an environmentally safe manner.

The mechanisms to implement these goals are somewhat limited. However, the statute does empower the EPA to develop and implement a strategy to promote source reduction; to provide grants to the states to implement source-reduction policies; and to create a database (the Source Reduction Clearinghouse) containing information on source reduction. The Act also imposes additional disclosure requirements to firms that were already required to report toxic chemical inventories under the Emergency Planning and Community Right-to-Know Act of 1986; under the Pollution Prevention Act, such firms must also file a report explaining their source reduction and recycling efforts over the previous year.

Although the Pollution Prevention Act is often thought of as lacking teeth, some other federal statutes do include enforceable policies promoting pollution prevention.* For example, the Resource Conservation and Recovery Act includes a variety of enforceable requirements for generators of hazardous waste to create plans to reduce the amount of waste produced.

* The EPA maintains a list of federal statutes mandating pollution prevention at www.epa.gov/p2/pollution-prevention-law-and-policies.

Federal vs. State Role in Pollution Control

Generally speaking, the federal government manages pollution that crosses state lines, whereas states are responsible for handling pollution problems within their own borders. Localities also play a role in managing localized pollution, such as storm water runoff and municipal trash management. However, the lines between interstate, state, and local pollution are not always easily drawn.

In many contexts—as, for example, with air pollution under the Clean Air Act—cooperative federalism structures support federal and state government actors in working together to address pollution. Such structures allow for significant variation at the state level in strategies for implementing federal requirements and for exceeding minimum standards. As a result, there can sometimes be significant variation in how pollution is managed below the federal level. For example, California has significantly stricter air pollution standards than those articulated by the federal EPA under the Clean Air Act.

Notwithstanding the possibility of important state and local variation in implementation and enforcement of pollution control measures, this book tends to focus on federal-level action when discussing U.S. pollution control. While we believe this emphasis provides the clearest way of understanding environmental law as it works across the United States, this should not be understood to suggest that U.S. pollution policy only works top-down, and never bottom-up. There are a number of situations in which the legal actions of one of the fifty quasi-sovereign states have national (or even international) implications. This is particularly true for larger states, such as California or Texas, which operate as significant global economies in their own right, though it can also occur with smaller states.

Though we will focus on federal action throughout the bulk of this chapter, it is important not to forget the background variance introduced by the individual states. An example is in order. One such example, both of significant state impact and unusual state procedure,

CALIFORNIA PROPOSITION 65 WARNING

WARNING: This product contains chemicals known to the State of
California to cause cancer and birth defects or other reproductive harm.

Figure 4. California Proposition 65—Warning for Toxic
Substances.

is California's Proposition 65. California has a special legal mechanism
called a "voter referendum" that allows specific legal propositions to be
included on a ballot. California voters then vote on the proposition, and
if a majority vote in favor, the proposition becomes law, without direct
involvement of the state legislature. In 1986, California voters approved
an initiative called the "Safe Drinking Water and Toxic Enforcement
Act of 1986," now commonly known as "Proposition 65" (figure 4). The
proposition addressed toxic chemical exposure by requiring the state
to publish a list of chemicals known to cause cancer, birth defects, or
other reproductive harm. Companies that do business in California
must include a "clear and reasonable" warning to potential purchasers
that the product includes a chemical on the list, which has grown to
include over eight hundred substances.

Proposition 65 plays a role in the regulation of toxic substances in
products throughout the country, and in some cases even internationally, by requiring labeling of products that contain substances known to
be carcinogenic or to cause reproductive harm. Because California is
the sixth-largest economy in the world, many businesses based in California also label their products sold elsewhere. As a result, "Proposition
65" labels on products are common throughout the United States, and
in some products sold internationally. This provides an example of how
California state law affects the regulation of toxic substances far beyond
its own borders.

States can also play an important role in national pollution control
by acting as parties to lawsuits. One state can sue another state in federal court, and indeed state suits for public nuisance—which are based

on the claim that action in another state is unreasonably infringing on the rights of the public in the suing state—played an important role historically in the development of U.S. pollution control laws.

The Roles of the Branches of Government in Pollution Control

Each branch of the government has different powers and responsibilities in managing pollution control.

LEGISLATIVE ROLE IN POLLUTION CONTROL

Legislatures pass environmental statutes that direct agencies and other actors on how to manage pollution. At the federal level, this includes specific statutes directed toward particular types of pollution, as well as general policy statements, including the Pollution Prevention Act, which describes the general policy of the United States on pollution control. State legislatures also pass state environmental statutes.

JUDICIAL ROLE IN POLLUTION CONTROL

Courts are important actors in managing pollution through two functions. First, they provide a judicial backstop to polluting activity, allowing people who are harmed by pollution to sue for compensation and/ or for an injunction, which prevents the polluting activity from continuing. These lawsuits may arise under common law (as when a polluter is sued for causing a private or public nuisance) or under statutes (when a polluter is not in compliance with a statutory duty). Importantly, while the emphasis in U.S. environmental law has shifted in recent years to environmental statutes and the administrative implementation of those statutes, common law remedies often still exist alongside statutory and regulatory law. Second, courts review agency actions related to pollution, to ensure that agency actions are constitutional, are within the agency's statutory authority, and follow prescribed, reasonable procedures. While the most influential pollution control statutes are federal, state courts also play important roles in managing state comme law claims, reviewing the actions of state agencies, and interpreting state environmental statutes.

EXECUTIVE ROLE IN POLLUTION CONTROL

The most important executive power in the United States for the purpose of pollution control is the executive's control of the administrative state. This includes the authority to direct how agencies make decisions, when those directions do not conflict with statutes. For example, every President from Reagan to Trump has directed that agencies should use cost-benefit analysis when permitted by statute. The President also plays an important role in priority setting, in large part through the appointment (and potential firing of) agency heads. While these types of prioritizations can be important, Presidents do not have the authority to direct agencies to disregard constitutionally enacted statutes. This acts as a check on the President's ability to control agency action. Finally, Presidents have the power to sign international treaties, though those treaties must be ratified by Congress before taking effect. Some Presidents have used this power to enter into pollution control treaties, as with the Great Lakes Water Quality Agreement, a commitment between the United States and Canada to protect the water quality of the Great Lakes.

AGENCIES' ROLE IN POLLUTION CONTROL

Agencies play a critical role in pollution control at the federal, state, and local levels. At the federal level, while a number of agencies have authority under specific statutes, the EPA serves as the most important institutional actor, and it often coordinates action even where states or other agencies are involved in implementation. It also serves as the home for significant research on environmental risk assessment, including a number of databases that collate useful scientific information related to pollutants or polluting activity. For example, the Integrated Risk Information System provides dose-response data on hundreds of regulated substances, and the Toxics Release Inventory chronicles a searchable database of releases of toxic substances, including where, when, what, and how much of a substance was released.

The EPA has a number of offices that are directed specifically toward pollution control, including the large Office of Air and Radiation; the Office of Chemical Safety and Pollution Prevention; and the Office of Water. The EPA's Office of Enforcement and Compliance Assurance also plays an important role in enforcing pollution control statutes. Other important agencies for pollution control include the Department of Energy's Office of Environmental Management, which addresses the problem of nuclear waste; the Department of the Interior's Office of Surface Mining Reclamation and Enforcement (OSMRE), which is responsible for mining-related pollution; and the Occupational Safety and Health Administration, which is responsible for managing occupational exposures to pollutants.

State environmental agencies are also central in implementing and enforcing both federal and state pollution control statutes.[2] Furthermore, local agencies often influence pollution control policies, particularly through zoning decisions, which can have important impacts on how populations are exposed to industrial and transport-related pollution.

DISCUSSION QUESTIONS

1. Should one government actor control pollution? Is federal or state government better suited to set pollution standards?
2. Should voters and nongovernment actors have more say in pollution standards?

LEGAL SNAPSHOTS:
POLLUTION CONTROL IN THE UNITED STATES

The next sections provide a series of "snapshots" explaining how the United States regulates five types of pollution: air pollution, water pollution, soil pollution, toxic substances, and waste.

Other types of pollution exist, including light pollution, noise pollution, and aesthetic pollution. The latter are highly local in impact, and in the United States each is managed by local authorities, most often by zoning boards. State common law also offers a general remedy where the use of property rises to the level of a nuisance, as can be the case with some forms of light, noise, or aesthetic pollution. Because these cases require a fact-specific inquiry, and are handled on the basis of individual state laws, they are not part of the snapshots provided in this primer.

AIR POLLUTION
DEFINITION

Air pollution is the contamination of air by materials or substances that are present at higher-than-normal concentrations, and which may have adverse effects on humans or on nonhuman organisms.[3]

DISTINCTIVE CHALLENGES OF REGULATING
AIR POLLUTION

One of the primary challenges of air pollution comes from its high stakes: it is by far the deadliest type of pollution in the United States, as it is in most of the world. Indeed, EPA studies suggest that air pollution imperils hundreds of thousands of U.S. lives each year.[4] The grave stakes of these health risks place additional pressure on scientific research about the expected impact of air pollutants.

Air pollution levels and types vary significantly across the United States. Generally speaking, air pollution is worst in areas that are heavily populated (including the Northeast and Southern California) and where industry is concentrated (including the traditionally industrial "Rust Belt" surrounding the Great Lakes). That said, geography can also play an important role in air pollution: cities near mountain ranges, for example, may experience higher levels of air pollution even where air pollution controls are stringent, simply because pollution that is emitted has nowhere to escape.

Air pollution is typically characterized by high mobility—many forms of air pollution drift with the wind—and by difficulties in detection, given that most air pollutants are not detectable by an untrained observer. As a result, the behaviors that cause air pollution may not be easily connected to their consequences and therefore may be harder to regulate. They can also be harder to control by individuals, who have fewer options for reducing exposures and must rely primarily on government action to regulate air quality.

There are many different types of air pollution, which means that regulatory challenges often vary with the source and type of the pollution. Some air pollution sources, like power plants or chemical plants, are stationary and concentrated. Regulating these sources often requires management of significant quantities of concentrated pollutants, and may also implicate the challenging informational burdens of attempting to regulate mixtures. On the bright side, the stationary nature of such sources means that polluting behaviors are relatively easy to identify, regulate, and measure. Nonstationary sources, like cars or lawnmowers, may lead to greater diffusion in pollution, and thus to greater challenges in even identifying relevant sources, and even greater challenges in measurement and enforcement. Furthermore, different air pollutants can have a wide range of effects on the human and nonhuman environment. In the case of some pollutants, only prolonged exposure at high levels has a noticeable effect. Other pollutants create immediate and highly harmful consequences and may require more immediate regulatory action. Finally, highly hazardous air pollutants, which can be expected to cause cancer, birth defects, or even sudden death, implicate many of the same challenges as general regulation of toxic substances.

KEY U.S. LEGAL APPROACHES TO AIR POLLUTION

The most important law on air pollution in the United States is the Clean Air Act, a sprawling statute that (with amendments) extends over almost a thousand pages and that is sometimes compared in complexity to the U.S. tax code.[5] This snapshot will discuss the key provisions of the Act, as well as the tort of nuisance, which continues to operate as a judicial backstop for air pollution control. For more detailed coverage of particular control measures or the regulation of particular industries, it is worth turning to the rich set of air pollution resources provided by the EPA.[6]

Clean Air Act and EPA Regulations

The Clean Air Act of 1970 (CAA) is a complex and detailed statute that has been amended multiple times. Administered by the EPA, the CAA is structured on the basis of a cooperative federalist partnership between the U.S. government and state and local governments. Under this approach, the federal EPA is generally responsible for setting minimum air quality standards, while states are responsible for determining how to implement those standards. States often have the authority to require more stringent air quality standards, but they are not permitted to have weaker standards.

The CAA is commonly viewed as one of the central achievements of U.S. environmental law. In 1990, amendments to the Act required the EPA to conduct scientifically reviewed studies of the impact of the Act on public health, economy, and environment in the United States. On the basis of these studies, the EPA predicts that the Act will prevent 230,000 early deaths a year in 2020, and estimates that the benefits of the Act exceed the costs of implementing it by thirty to one.[7]

Within the CAA, the National Ambient Air Quality Standards are widely viewed as the centerpiece of U.S. air pollution control. The CAA also outlines a number of additional and important regimes for dealing with different aspects of air pollution, including different requirements for existing and new sources of pollution, for mobile and stationary sources, for particularly hazardous air pollutants (such as those that are known to cause cancer), and for interstate and international air pollution.

NATIONAL AMBIENT AIR QUALITY STANDARDS

The National Ambient Air Quality Standards (NAAQS) regulate the quantity of key common air pollutants—called "criteria pollutants"—that are suspended in the outdoor air anywhere in the United States (table 5). The EPA regulates criteria pollutants by developing science-based criteria for setting permissible levels. There are two types of standards for criteria pollutants: primary standards and secondary standards. Primary standards provide public health protection, which includes protecting sensitive populations (such as children, the elderly, and asthmatics). Secondary standards protect welfare and the environment, which has been interpreted to include damage to animals, crops, vegetation, and property.

Somewhat unusually for the United States, the NAAQS are precautionary: primary standards must be set at levels "requisite to protect the public health" with an "adequate margin of safety." Furthermore, and even more unusually for the United States, the Supreme Court has interpreted the CAA to mean that NAAQS must be set *only* by reference to health, and without any consideration of cost.[8] As a result, the EPA is actually prevented from using cost-benefit analysis—which is so influential in so many of its regulations—in setting the stringency of the NAAQS.

If the Administrator of the EPA finds that a pollutant causes or contributes to human health risks—a so-called "endangerment finding"—the CAA requires the EPA to regulate that pollutant. This portion of the statute was famously used in the 2007 Supreme Court case *Massachusetts v. EPA* to require the EPA to evaluate whether greenhouse gases pose a threat to human health or the environment. In 2009, the

TABLE 5

National Ambient Air Quality Standards

Criteria Pollutant	Description and Common Source(s) in Air	Health Impacts	Maximum Level (Primary Standard)
Carbon monoxide (CO)	This colorless, odorless gas is commonly released by burning fossil fuels (e.g., fuel for cars and trucks or fossil-fuel-based energy generation).	Breathing CO reduces the amount of oxygen inhaled, so can cause dizziness and confusion in low doses and unconsciousness or death in high doses.	9 ppm (averaged over 8 hours) or 35 ppm (over 1 hour)
Lead (Pb)	Lead is a naturally occurring element that was introduced to the air in substantial quantities by leaded gasoline; modern sources include ore processing, waste incinerators, utilities, and smelters.	Lead (whether inhaled or otherwise consumed) becomes distributed throughout the body in the blood, and accumulates in the bones. It has a number of health impacts, including neurological impacts on children (such as lowered IQ) and cardiovascular effects in adults.	0.15 µg/m3 (averaged over 3 months)
Nitrogen dioxide (NO$_2$)	Nitrogen dioxide (like other nitrogen oxides, NO$_x$) is a highly reactive gas that primarily enters the air from the burning of fuel. Nitrogen oxides also react with other chemicals in the air to form particulate matter and ozone.	Short-term exposures can irritate airways in the human respiratory system, aggravating respiratory conditions like asthma. Longer-term exposures contribute to development of asthma and respiratory infection.	100 ppb (averaged over 1 hour) or 53 ppb (averaged over 1 year)
Ozone (O$_3$)	Ground-level ozone is not directly emitted into the air; rather, it is created by interactions between nitrogen oxides (NO$_x$) and volatile organic compounds (VOCs) in the presence of heat and sunlight. It is most likely to reach unhealthy levels in sunny, warm urban environments.	When at ground level, high levels of ozone generate smog and can cause a variety of health impacts, particularly on the respiratory system; these are particularly dangerous for people with preexisting respiratory conditions like asthma. At the atmospheric level, ozone provides an environmental benefit by screening the Earth from ultraviolet radiation from the Sun.	0.07 ppm (averaged over 8 hours)

TABLE 5 *(continued)*

Criteria Pollutant	Description and Common Source(s) in Air	Health Impacts	Maximum Level (Primary Standard)
Particulate matter (PM)	Particulate matter, or "particle pollution," is a mixture of small liquid and solid particles suspended in air. Different types of particles have different sources. Coarser particles, such as those with a diameter less than 10 microns (PM_{10}), include soot, dirt, and dust. Fine particles, including particles less than 2.5 micrometers in diameter ($PM_{2.5}$), result from a variety of different sources and chemical processes, including from interactions of nitrogen oxides (NO_x) with other substances.	Particulate matter contains microscopic particles that are so small that they can be inhaled and cause serious health problems, particularly to respiratory systems. Inhaled particles can get deep into the lungs, and some may even enter the bloodstream; fine particles are particularly likely to penetrate deeply into bodily systems, and thus pose the greatest risk to human health. Fine particles are also the main cause of reduced visibility (haze) in parts of the United States.	For $PM_{2.5}$: 12.0 µg/m^3 (averaged over 1 year) For PM_{10}: 35 µg/m^3 (averaged over 24 hours)
Sulfur dioxide (SO_2)	Sulfur is a naturally occuring element; sulfur dioxide enters the air as a result of burning either sulfur or materials containing sulfur, such as coal. Sulfur oxides can also react with other substances to form small particles, contributing to PM pollution.	Short-term exposure to SO_2 can harm the respiratory system and make breathing difficult, particularly for those with respiratory disease like asthma.	75 ppb (averaged over 1 hour)

EPA made a formal endangerment finding for greenhouse gases, making their regulation by the EPA a legal requirement under the CAA.[9]

The EPA sets NAAQS for six criteria pollutants: ground-level ozone, particulate matter,[10] carbon monoxide, lead, sulfur dioxide, and nitrogen dioxide. For each standard, the EPA identifies an averaging time, a method of calculating the average, and a level, which is expressed either in parts of the pollutant per million (ppm) or billion (ppb) or as a measure of the weight of the pollutant suspended in each cubic meter of air (µg/m^3). Of these six criteria pollutants, the EPA views particulate matter and ground-level ozone as the most widespread health threats. Notably, since the CAA was passed in 1970, the EPA reports that aggregate emissions of these six pollutants has dropped by 70 percent.[11]

While the federal EPA sets primary and secondary NAAQS, states are responsible for developing State Implementation Plans (commonly called SIPs) to spell out how the air quality standards will be met. This allows states to decide how many emissions to allocate to particular industries or uses. Once developed, SIPs are submitted to the EPA for approval. If a state fails to submit a plan that complies with the NAAQS, the EPA can substitute a Federal Implementation Plan (FIP). The EPA also develops FIPs for Indian tribal lands if tribes elect not to create their own plans. Currently, the EPA administers ten FIPs around the country. States are also tasked with monitoring and enforcing specific emissions standards once set. Since the Clean Air Act Amendments of 1990, Indian tribes have authority similar to that of states in regulating their air quality, and may present Tribal Implementation Plans (TIPs) or choose to have FIPs implemented instead.

Areas that meet the primary requirements of the NAAQS are called *attainment* areas; areas that do not meet the primary standards are called *nonattainment* areas. An area may be in attainment for one criteria pollutant (e.g., sulfur dioxide) and in nonattainment for another (e.g., carbon monoxide). Attainment status typically applies at the county level.

Attainment status matters because sources of pollution in nonattainment areas are subject to additional requirements; it can be difficult or even impossible for a new source of pollution to open up or expand in nonattainment areas, even if there are significant non-environmental benefits to its creation. The EPA keeps a publicly available database updated with attainment status throughout the country,[12] and a website that members of the public can check at any time to know current air quality and to be warned about attendant risks.[13] More than a third of the U.S. population (123 million people) live in areas in nonattainment for at least one criteria pollutant.[14] About a quarter of these (34 million people) live in California.[15]

NEW AND GRANDFATHERED SOURCES
OF AIR POLLUTION

One of the most important—and most criticized—aspects of the CAA is that, when it was enacted in 1970, it did not require existing stationary sources to comply with new regulations promoting the NAAQS until (or unless) those plants were modified or upgraded in a way that would increase air pollution. These "grandfathered" sources were expected to eventually become obsolete, or to be forced to update. Instead, many sources found ways to continue operating long beyond their original expected lifetimes. Their management remains a source of challenge in the United States today.[16]

MOBILE SOURCES

The CAA manages air pollution from mobile sources (including cars, trucks, buses, and nonroad equipment) through a variety of different tools. Among other strategies, it requires manufacturers to build cleaner engines; requires refiners to produce cleaner fuels; encourages development and sale of alternative fuels; requires areas with air pollution problems to run inspection and maintenance programs for their vehicles; and requires the EPA to issue rules to reduce mobile source pollution, including by setting vehicle exhaust standards. Since the EPA first set emissions standards, emissions from new cars have been reduced by over 90 percent. One early and important use of the CAA was the EPA's decision to begin phasing out lead in gasoline (added to help engine performance) in the mid-1970s because it was found to have important health impacts, particularly for children. Leaded gasoline was banned entirely in 1996, as a result of EPA implementation of the CAA's mobile source requirements.

HAZARDOUS AIR POLLUTANTS

Particularly dangerous air pollutants ("Hazardous Air Pollutants," or HAPs) are regulated under amendments to the CAA passed in 1990. Unlike the common criteria air pollutants, which are regulated under the NAAQS and much of the rest of the CAA, HAPs—pollutants "known or suspected to cause cancer or other serious health effects, such as reproductive effects or birth defects, or adverse environmental effects"—may originate from only one or a few industrial sources.

Because HAPs pose significant health threats that generally originate from a few, relatively identifiable sources, the CAA applies a different regulatory structure than it uses for criteria pollutants. Rather than using an ambient standard (such as those set in the NAAQS), HAPs are primarily regulated using technology-based emissions standards. The EPA publishes a list of industrial sources ("source categories") that emit HAPs, such as dry cleaners, gas stations, or iron and steel foundries. The EPA then promulgates regulations for these sources as emissions standards (called the National Emission Standards for Hazardous Air Pollutants).[17] Larger "major" sources must comply with a stricter technology-based standard, called the Maximum Achievable Control Technology, while smaller sources may comply with less stringent requirements. Importantly, HAP standards apply to existing as well as new sources of pollution.

ACID RAIN AND CROSS-STATE MARKET TRADING SCHEMES

Historically, the United States has depended heavily on coal-fired power plants for its electricity needs. Burning coal generates sulfur dioxide and nitrogen oxides—criteria air pollutants that cause acidification of soil and water when they bond with water and fall as acid rain. Management of these pollutants formed the basis for some of the earliest air pollution judicial cases, as in the famous 1907 case *Georgia v. Tennessee Copper*,[18] in which Georgia sued a Tennessee smelter for creating "sulphurous acid gas."

In 1990, the CAA was amended to control acid rain by creating a new market-based approach to emissions of sulfur dioxide—the world's first large-scale application of cap and trade in pollution control. Under the sulfur dioxide trading scheme, rather than prescribing how emitters (particularly power plants) would reduce emissions, the EPA distributed pollution allowances. Emitters could then choose to use their allowances, to reduce their emissions and sell their permits on the national emissions trading market, or to buy more permits along with the right to emit more sulfur dioxide. Although some "hot spots" remained where emissions were concentrated, in general, the trading program reduced acid rain substantially throughout much of the country; by 2007, annual emissions had declined by 43 percent from 1990 levels, despite electricity generation from coal-fired power plants increasing by a quarter over the same period, and one study suggests that the mortality rate declined by as much as 5 percent as a result of the policy.[19] In subsequent years, building on the success of the sulfur dioxide trading regime, the EPA has created additional trading systems, including one for interstate transport of nitrogen oxides, via the Cross-State Air Pollution Rule.[20]

INTERSTATE AND INTERNATIONAL AIR POLLUTION

Because air pollution is so mobile, it can easily pass state or national borders, posing a risk of interstate or international air pollution. In addition to the cross-state trading schemes mentioned above, the CAA has several other mechanisms intended to reduce long-range transport of air pollution from one area to another, and particularly to help address the risk that a downwind state ends up in nonattainment because of an upwind state's emissions. These include giving the EPA the authority to require states (or tribes) to develop plans to address downwind pollution, or even to take over with a FIP if no such plan is forthcoming or appropriate; providing for the creation of interstate commissions to develop regional strategies for cleaning up air pollution; and requiring the EPA to work with states to reduce regional haze that affects visibility in national parks and wilderness areas (such as the Grand Canyon and Yosemite).

Interestingly, the CAA also includes a section for addressing international air pollution. That section (§ 119) applies where the Administrator of the EPA finds that there is an endangerment of public health or welfare in foreign countries from pollution emitted in the United States, and where foreign countries have given the United States reciprocal air-pollution-prevention rights. This provision has never been invoked to address international air pollution in the United States—despite the significant cross-border impacts of conventional pollutants, particularly with respect to Canada and Mexico, and the significant U.S. contribution to climate change.

The United States is also a signatory on several air pollution treaties, though these are not generally viewed as a central part of U.S. domestic air pollution policy. Nevertheless, they include the U.S.-Mexico Border 2020 Program and the U.S.-Canada Air Quality Agreement. The EPA is responsible for implementing both treaties.[21]

Nuisance Law and Tort Claims for Air Pollution

Prior to the CAA, control of air pollution was mostly effected through common law nuisance actions. Individuals might sue in private nuisance, claiming that another's behavior unreasonably interfered with their property right. However, even when plaintiffs won, they might only be awarded damages.[22] Only in unusual cases, as where states successfully brought a claim in public nuisance, were injunctions on polluting activity occasionally awarded.[23]

Today, the CAA provides the primary legal regime for regulating air quality in the United States. Nevertheless, the common law continues to provide a judicial backstop for states or parties harmed by some kinds of air pollution. Importantly, in *American Electric Power Co. v. Connecticut* (2011), the U.S. Supreme Court held that the CAA displaces federal common law public nuisance claims against carbon dioxide emitters. But state tort claims (including in nuisance, negligence, and trespass) against in-state emitters may still be viable.[24]

The United States was also involved in the seminal *Trail Smelter* case, a transboundary air pollution case in which a Canadian smelter was damaging U.S. agriculture, and in which the foundational "harm principle" in international law was developed. The case has had limited impact on domestic U.S. law but remains a touchstone in international environmental law.[25]

TAKEAWAYS

✓ Air pollution poses distinctive challenges to control for many reasons, including its high stakes, high mobility, difficulties in detection, and the variety of types and sources of air pollutants.

✓ The intricate Clean Air Act is the centerpiece of U.S. air pollution control policy. It is expected to prevent 230,000 premature deaths per year by 2020.

✓ Under the CAA, the EPA sets National Ambient Air Quality Standards for common "criteria pollutants." Although the standards are set federally, states decide how to achieve the standards. New sources (and modified old sources) generally face far more stringent regulation than sources that were grandfathered in when the Act was passed.

✓ The CAA contains a series of additional regimes for controlling specific types of pollution, including for mobile sources, hazardous air pollutants, and acid rain.

✓ State common law and international law remain potential backstops for air pollution claims, though these are far less influential than the CAA.

✓ The CAA also plays a critical role in U.S. regulation of greenhouse gases (as discussed in chapter 8).

DISCUSSION QUESTIONS

1. The NAAQS require that the same air quality be achieved across the United States. Does it make sense to have the same standards for air quality across a country, regardless of the difficulty of achieving those standards or differences in population or sensitivity of ecosystem?

2. What advantages or disadvantages are there in allowing states—as local authorities—to decide how to implement air pollution laws?

3. How would you determine what an adequate margin of safety is for air pollution?

4. Why do you think legislators might have chosen to grandfather in old sources of air pollution? Is it fair to apply laxer standards to old sources and more stringent standards to new sources?

WATER POLLUTION
DEFINITION

Water pollution is the contamination of water by materials that are out of place or that are present at higher-than-normal concentrations, and which may have adverse effects on humans or on nonhuman organisms.

DISTINCTIVE CHALLENGES OF REGULATING WATER POLLUTION

The first key challenge in the management of water pollution is the diversity of uses for water. It is a resource for drinking, for agriculture, and for industry. It is used to cool power plants, as a habitat and a medium for transport, for recreation, and for exploiting other resources, such as fish. These diverse uses create additional complexity for water pollution policy, because substances and conditions that constitute pollution for one type of use may be desirable or even a precondition for another.

A second key challenge comes from the wide variety of behaviors that can create water pollution. Some of these behaviors are concentrated (as with industrial emissions from a pipe into a river) and some are quite diffuse (as with littering, applying fertilizer, or washing cars). At the same time, water can become polluted from characteristics or events in the non-human environment—for example, contamination of well water by naturally high levels of soil arsenic in the Pacific Northwest, or where beavers introduce *Giardia* into a stream. This means that regulatory regimes to address water pollution must find ways to address many types of human behavior, while simultaneously managing complex natural processes.

A third challenge comes from two specific hydrogeological and chemical properties of water. First, water (and therefore the pollution it carries) is at least somewhat mobile. This creates geographic distance, sometimes vast, between the source of water pollution and its impacts. Second, when water is moving, it tends to channel itself into recurring pathways that are generally unidirectional. This means, in many cases, that pollution relationships are similarly unidirectional: upstream (or upcurrent) actors can pollute the water for downstream actors, but downstream actors have no reciprocal opportunity to pollute. This can create bargaining problems and distributional issues between polluter and pollutee, especially where downstream pollution accumulates from multiple upstream emissions. These challenges are particularly pronounced in the southward-flowing Mississippi River and in the Gulf of Mexico, into which much of U.S. agricultural land drains.

Finally, there are distinctive distributional challenges related to pollution of drinking water. While drinking water is generally of high quality in the United States, it is most likely to contain significant pollutants in cities and areas with aging pipes. Drinking water can also be obtained through private markets, including bottled water and home filtering, which can create distributional and environmental justice concerns. The latter options are available only to wealthier people, which raises questions of the appropriate quality standards for drinking water and what the conditions for access and use should be. This becomes particularly relevant in areas of relative scarcity where people may want to use drinking water to irrigate gardens or for other nonessential uses, putting additional pressure on a scarce resource.

KEY U.S. LEGAL APPROACHES TO WATER POLLUTION

Federal water pollution law is dominated by the ambitious Clean Water Act (CWA). Other statutes, including the Safe Drinking Water Act and the Ocean Dumping Act, apply to particular uses and behaviors affecting water pollution. The EPA is the primary regulatory authority for most federal water pollution control, although states play a continued vital role, particularly in managing nonpoint source water pollution, and other agencies coordinate with the EPA in managing marine pollution.

Clean Water Act

The CWA is the most important federal water pollution statute in the United States.[26] The CWA is administered by the federal EPA and applies to all surface waters of the United States. The Act does not apply to groundwater—the water present beneath the earth's surface—or to questions of water quantity.[27]

The CWA is an ambitious statute that aims "to restore and maintain the chemical, physical, and biological integrity of the nation's waters."[28] The statute also articulates a national policy of attempting to secure zero discharge of pollutants, and water quality that is "fishable" and "swimmable." Initially these goals were intended to be accomplished by 1985 and 1983, respectively.

To further these goals, the Act established two foundational regulatory schemes. First, it prohibited any discharge of any pollutant into the waters of the United States without a permit. The related permitting system—the National Pollutant Discharge Elimination System (NPDES)—allows dischargers to emit pollutants only when doing so cannot be prevented by the "best" technologies (though what constitutes "best" technologies is controversial and commonly litigated). Importantly, the NPDES applies only to discharges of pollution by so-called "point sources"—stationary concentrated sources, such as industrial pipes that drain into a river, or municipal wastewater systems—to the exclusion of diffuse "nonpoint sources," such as storm water drainage, most agricultural sources, or litter. Nonpoint sources like these are primarily regulated by states and localities. This is an important limitation, as the EPA estimates that nonpoint sources are now responsible for the majority of water quality impairments in the United States.[29]

The second critical regulatory scheme in the CWA consists of its mechanisms for attempting to achieve fishable/swimmable standards. To this end, the statute establishes a set relationship between state and federal authorities. States are required to establish Water Quality Standards (WQS), which consist of a designated use (such as water supply, recreation, industrial, or other) and a statement (either numerical or narrative) identifying maximum concentrations of various pollutants that would not interfere with the designated use. States retain substantial discretion in setting WQS, and water quality continues to vary significantly across states.

The CWA remains relatively controversial, and argument continues about whether and to what extent it has succeeded at its lofty goals. Even decades after the Act was passed, over half of U.S. waterways violate state water quality standards[30]—though defenders have noted that water quality was even worse before the CWA. One commonly cited piece of anecdotal evidence is that the Cuyahoga River—which famously caught on fire in 1969, as it had every decade for a century—has had no fires since the passage of the CWA in 1972.[31]

Another source of continuing controversy relates to the scope of the CWA, which applies only to the "waters of the United States" (WOTUS). Because of the hydrogeological properties of water, water often travels between states—a fact that grounds federal jurisdiction over water pollution. Yet some water—such as water in seasonal wetlands—has a more attenuated relationship to interstate waters. In some such cases, the Supreme Court has limited the reach of the CWA.[32]

Coastal and Marine Pollution

Generally speaking, the CWA is presumed to apply to discharges into coastal and oceanic waters. Point source discharges into ocean waters are thus subject to the NPDES permitting regime. This has had a limited effect on U.S. coastal water quality, however, as most marine and coastal pollution originates with nonpoint sources, including urban and agricultural runoff. Atmospheric deposition of pollutants that lead to ocean acidification are also treated as nonpoint sources of pollution. As a result, management of the majority of coastal and oceanic pollution is generally left to the states, and has faced substantial challenges.[33] That said, the EPA and other federal agencies do play a more central role in some limited forms of coastal and marine pollution control. For example, the Beaches Environmental Assessment and Coastal Health (BEACH) Act, which amended the Clean Water Act in 2000, addresses a particular risk of marine water pollution: namely, the risk of disease to users of the nation's coastal recreation waters. It operates via two primary mechanisms: a series of grants to state and local authorities to help fund improved monitoring of water quality, and the creation of a national informational database—the Beach Advisory and Closing Online Notification System—to provide publicly available information about pollution occurrences at national beaches.[34] Another example is the Oil Pollution Act of 1990, which also amended the CWA and which addresses the problem of oil pollution—including oil spills—in U.S. waters. The Act created additional liability for those responsible for oil spills, including by allowing for "natural resource damages" to account for damage to the natural environment. It also created an Oil Spill Liability Trust Fund (financed by a tax on oil) to fund cleanup when those responsible are unable to do so.

Finally, another important part of the U.S. approach to marine pollution is the Marine Protection, Research and Sanctuaries Act (MPRSA), also known as the Ocean Dumping Act. The Act prohibits dumping into the ocean any material that would unreasonably degrade or endanger human health or the marine environment. Like the CWA, it prohibits such discharges without a permit. The Act spreads statutory responsibilities across four agencies—the EPA, the U.S. Army Corps of Engineers, the U.S. Coast Guard, and the National Oceanic and Atmospheric Administration (NOAA). Generally speaking, the EPA is responsible for issuing most permits for ocean dumping (except for dumping of dredged materials), the Army Corps of Engineers manages permits for dredged materials, the U.S. Coast Guard provides surveillance and enforcement, and NOAA performs long-term research on the impacts of marine pollution.

Notably—and unusually among U.S. environmental statutes—the Act implements the requirements of an international agreement: the Convention on the Prevention of Marine Pollution by Dumping of Wastes and Other Matter of 1972, also known as the London Convention.

Safe Drinking Water Act

The Safe Drinking Water Act (SDWA) is the primary law for protecting public drinking water from contamination. The Act applies to the 170,000 privately and publicly owned water systems in the United States that provide piped water for human consumption. It does not apply to bottled water, which is regulated by the Food and Drug Administration.

As with the CWA, the SDWA is administered by the federal EPA, with implementation and enforcement delegated to the states. The SDWA requires the EPA to promulgate national drinking water regulations for contaminants that may pose health risks and that are likely to be present in public drinking water—around ninety contaminants as of this writing. The regulation of each contaminant requires the EPA to engage in a multipart process. The first step is the identification of a safe level of contamination by setting a "maximum contaminant level goal" (MCLG). This is the level at which no known human health effects occur, which allows an adequate margin of safety. The second step involves the setting of an enforceable standard—a maximum contaminant level—that is as close to the aspirationally safe MCLG as "feasible," using best technology, and taking costs into account. The statute thus explicitly requires the EPA to rely on risk assessment in setting these levels, and to use the best available science. States are responsible for implementing the requirements of the SDWA via local public drinking water systems.

Though the quality in most U.S. drinking water systems is high, when problems arise, the impact can be serious. One common problem relates to the presence of lead or copper in plumbing materials, including in pipes that carry water from the water main into homes and buildings. Congress did not ban use of lead in such service lines until 1986, and millions of homes are still served by lead service lines around the country. EPA has struggled to find effective ways to address this concern; its Lead and Copper Rule, issued in 1991, has been increasingly criticized in light of the drinking water crisis in Flint, Michigan (as well as similar crises in other locations), where the majority Black population was exposed to dangerous levels of lead as a result of corrosion in leaded supply lines.

The SDWA also provides the primary body of federal law concerning groundwater pollution; federal groundwater protections apply to aquifers and wellheads and include a funding provision to help states pay for groundwater initiatives. That said, states retain significant authority over the quality of their groundwater, which many small communities continue to rely on as their main source of drinking water.

Section 1421 of the SDWA also authorizes establishment of state "underground injection control" programs to protect underground sources of water; these programs have come under additional pressure in recent years with the rise of hydraulic fracturing ("fracking") for oil and gas extraction. As of this writing, the statute delegates enforcement authority for oil and gas injection operations to the states, with very limited EPA oversight.

TAKEAWAYS

✓ Key challenges to water pollution control include the diversity of water uses, the variety of behaviors that can create water pollution (including both concentrated and diffuse uses), the fact that moving water tends to follow unidirectional channels, and, finally, the distributional challenges related to drinking water control.

✓ The Clean Water Act prohibits any point source discharge of a pollutant into the waterways of the United States without a permit. Point source water pollution is permitted only when it satisfies the "best" technology standard.

✓ Nonpoint source pollution of surface water is primarily regulated by states. States are also responsible for designating

the uses that determine whether water quality has been
successfully achieved.

✓ Coastal and marine pollution is managed through several
different statutory regimes, including the Clean Water Act, the
Ocean Dumping Act, and the Oil Pollution Act.

✓ Drinking water quality is regulated through a cooperative
relationship between federal law and state implementation. Under
the Safe Drinking Water Act, the EPA sets maximum contaminant
levels in drinking water as close to safe levels as is feasible, given
technological and cost constraints. States then implement these
requirements to protect their drinking water quality.

✓ Groundwater is largely regulated by the states, although there
are also some groundwater protection provisions in the SDWA.

DISCUSSION QUESTIONS

1. What does it mean to "restore and maintain the chemical,
   physical, and biological integrity of [a] nation's waters," as the
   Clean Water Act aims to do? How could policymakers know
   if they had achieved this goal? Are there good reasons for
   policymakers to adopt lofty environmental goals, even if they
   are challenging to measure or achieve?

2. Does it make sense to regulate point and nonpoint sources of
   water pollution differently? Are there strategies that could work
   in regulating both?

3. Should nonpoint sources be under federal control instead of
   state control? Why or why not?

4. Does it make sense for states to have so much control over
   water resources and water quality?

5. How safe should drinking water be? Does the SDWA
   distinction between "maximum contaminant goals" and
   "maximum contaminant levels" make sense?

6. Does it make sense to adopt different regulatory schemes for surface water and groundwater? For drinking water and other water?

SOIL POLLUTION
DEFINITION

Soil pollution is the contamination of soils by materials that are out of place or that are present at higher-than-normal concentrations, and which may have adverse effects on humans or on nonhuman organisms.

DISTINCTIVE CHALLENGES OF REGULATING SOIL POLLUTION

Soil pollution can accumulate from a variety of sources, including industrial and agricultural land uses. Common activities causing soil pollution include mining, activities of heavy industry, corrosion of underground storage tanks, intensive farming, and leaching from solid or liquid wastes. The most common chemicals involved are petroleum hydrocarbons, pesticides, heavy metals, and solvents. Importantly, while many soil pollutants originate with human behavior, it is also possible to have higher-than-normal concentrations of pollutants, such as arsenic, which occur naturally in some soils.

Soil formation is an extremely slow process, which makes soil essentially a nonrenewable resource. Soil can function as a habitat and provides many essential ecosystems services. The geographic distribution of soil pollution varies by type—linked, for example, to industrial activity, mining, agriculture, or urbanization. Apart from soil pollution in the traditional sense, there are also other activities that can damage soil and its ability to provide essential environmental functions. An example of this is soil sealing, where ground is covered with impermeable materials.

Because soil pollution becomes embedded in the affected soil, it can be expensive to remediate, requiring either removal or treatment of contaminated soil. In case of removal, the contaminated soil still has to be managed. Soil pollution also has a complex and interactive relationship with other media of pollution. It can cause air and water pollution—for example, where toxic chemicals in soil leach into groundwater, or where soil (naturally) contributes to air pollution by releasing volatile compounds through the decomposition of organic materials, or where contaminated soil is incinerated. At the same time, soil pollution can be caused by other forms of pollution—for example, where acid rain acidifies the soil or where agricultural runoff leads to high levels of nitrogen in the soil.

A final complicating factor is that certain concentrations of potentially damaging material can be beneficial for some soil uses. High-nitrogen additives, for example, can be highly beneficial to farmers as a fertilizer or, more generally, as "soil improvers." But when water runoff over high-nitrogen soils accumulates, it creates serious water quality problems, as happens in the Mississippi River. The trade-offs between the positive uses and harmful effects of these types of additives pose special challenges in setting soil pollution policy.

The geographic distribution of soil pollution varies by type. Industrial soil pollution exists primarily in places of (former) industry, including along the eastern seaboard and around the Great Lakes. Mining-related pollution is spread out across much of the country, but over two-thirds of U.S. coal production is centered in five states (Wyoming, West Virginia, Kentucky, Illinois, and Pennsylvania), and these states experience heightened pollution from coal extraction. Agricultural soil pollution is particularly prevalent in agricultural communities in the Midwest.

KEY U.S. LEGAL APPROACHES TO SOIL POLLUTION

The United States does not have any single legal actor tasked with managing soil pollution from all sources. Nevertheless, there are two key federal statutory regimes directed toward managing soil pollution: the

Comprehensive Environmental Response, Compensation, and Liability Act (CERCLA, aka Superfund), which deals with highly contaminated sites; and the Surface Mining Control and Reclamation Act (SMCRA), which addresses soil pollution from mining activities. These are each described in more detail below. Where soil pollution interacts with other pollution media—as where contaminated soil is incinerated, or runoff over contaminated soil generates water pollution—it is generally handled through statutory regimes that address those media.

There is also no overarching federal legal regime designated for managing agricultural soil pollution, despite its prevalence in much of the country's fertile lands. Instead, agricultural soil pollution is addressed through multiple statutory and regulatory regimes that focus on media other than soil, and through state and local regulation. The resulting set of regulations for any particular farm is quite complicated.[35] Relevant regimes include the CWA (for managing runoff), the Emergency Planning and Community Right-to-Know Act (for managing potentially dangerous spills), and the Resource Conservation and Recovery Act (for managing increased soil concentrations that make soil into "waste"), as well as a variety of state and local requirements.

Comprehensive Environmental Response, Compensation, and Liability Act

CERCLA was created to manage hazardous waste sites. Although such sites exist throughout the United States, there is a particular concentration in the maritime Northeast and in the "Rust Belt" surrounding the Great Lakes, where a significant amount of polluting industry was located historically.[36] Indeed, CERCLA was passed in the wake of substantial media coverage of one of these sites—Love Canal, a neighborhood near Niagara Falls, New York, that was built (unbeknownst to its residents) on a hazardous-waste dump site (see spotlight 14).

SPOTLIGHT 14. LOVE CANAL

During the 1940s, Love Canal—a neighborhood in Niagara Falls, New York—was the location of a landfill where the Hooker Chemical Company dumped over twenty thousand tons of chemical byproducts from the manufacturing of dyes, solvents, and synthetic resins. Upon closing the dump site in 1952, Hooker buried the waste under twenty feet of soil and covered the site with a clay seal to prevent leakage. Over time, vegetation grew on top of the site.

Hooker sold the land to a local school district in 1953. Infamously, prior to the sale, Hooker's attorney wrote to the company's president to suggest that selling the land could help alleviate future liability for cleanup of the contaminated site. The school board purchased the land for one dollar, and a school and a neighborhood were built on top of the site. During construction, building crews broke through the protective clay cap on top of the dump site. Subsequently, the school district sold surrounding land to private developers to build a new neighborhood of homes and apartment buildings.

New residents of Love Canal were not informed of the neighborhood's history as a chemical dump site, or the breakage of the protective seal, and there was no ongoing monitoring or evaluation of the chemical wastes stored underground. More than four hundred children attended the school sited on top of the dump site, and thousands of people lived in surrounding homes. Over time, residents began noticing black fluid flowing into adjacent land from the eponymous canal. After a wet winter in 1977 raised the nearby water table, the state environmental agency began investigating and found an abnormal incidence of miscarriages and other health problems in the neighborhood. National environmental reporters wrote a series of articles on the site, which became a national media event. President Jimmy Carter declared the site a national emergency on August 7, 1978. This was the first time in U.S. history that federal emergency funds were used for an event other than a natural disaster.

> National attention to Love Canal helped galvanize passage of CERCLA, and in 1981, Love Canal itself was one of the first sites added to the National Priorities List of contaminated sites for cleanup. Cleanup at the Love Canal site ended in 2004, after twenty-three years and total expenditure of some $400 million. The site has since been removed from the Superfund list, and many of the homes along the canal have been renovated and sold to new owners.

The most famous aspect of CERCLA is its creation of the "Super-fund." The fund was meant to help bear the significant costs associated with addressing soil contamination at hazardous waste sites, which rise to an average of $30 million per site—though large and highly contaminated sites, such as Love Canal, can cost even more. Congress initially funded the Superfund with $600 million toward remediating hazardous waste. Already by 1980, however, the EPA estimated that remediating known sites would cost over $44 billion. To make up the shortfall, CERCLA included a set of provisions designed to extract the costs of remediation from the private sector. Accordingly, CERCLA provides a broad set of liability provisions, which make parties with existing or past links to existing disposal sites—"potentially responsible parties"—potentially liable for cleanup costs. Controversially, this includes current and past owners of contaminated land, even if those owners did not participate in the polluting activity.[37] Contributions from potentially responsible parties are allocated in court, which means that actually recovering costs can take decades and involve very significant judicial process.

To decide which sites to address and in which order, CERCLA makes the EPA responsible for creating a National Priorities List for contaminated sites to determine which sites warrant further investigation and remediation, and a National Contingency Plan to outline procedures and standards for responding to releases of pollutants, and for managing the restoration process for sites identified as priorities. As of 2020, there are over thirteen hundred Superfund sites on the National Priorities List. Throughout the history of the program, a total of approximately four hundred sites have been cleaned up and removed from the list.

Surface Mining Control and Reclamation Act of 1977

The United States has substantial deposits of coal. In recent years, decreases in renewable energy costs and lowering natural gas costs from fracking have led the coal mining industry to decline. That said, coal is still mined in twenty-five of the fifty states, with five states— Wyoming, West Virginia, Kentucky, Illinois, and Pennsylvania— responsible for the production of more than 70 percent of U.S. coal.

SMCRA is the primary legal regime regulating the environmental impacts of coal mining. The Act was passed in 1977 in response to environmental concerns about the consequences of surface mining, which remains the primary method of coal mining in the United States.[38] Surface mining is also known as "strip" or "open-pit" mining, a process in which the soil and rock are removed to expose the mineral deposit.

SMCRA created the Office of Surface Mining Reclamation and Enforcement (OSMRE) as an agency within the Department of the Interior. The office is tasked with promulgating regulations for active coal mines and for reclaiming abandoned mine lands, as well as with ensuring consistency across state regulatory programs. Among other features, SMCRA includes an Abandoned Mine Land fund to pay for the cleanup of mines that were abandoned before the statute was passed. Notably, the fund is financed through a tax on mined coal. Higher tax rates are assigned to surface mining than to underground mining, which is generally associated with less soil pollution and related water pollution.

Like many other pollution control statutes, SMCRA is based on cooperative federalism, leaving states significant authority to regulate coal mining in their territory, with minimum baselines, enforcement, and coordination provided by the federal government. States can operate their own regulatory program under SMCRA if they can show the Office of

Surface Mining Reclamation and Enforcement (OSMRE) that state laws are at least as strict as SMCRA, and that the state has a regulatory agency that can operate a mining program. Alongside these state agencies, the federal government and OSMRE remain the key authority for public lands (on which approximately 40 percent of mining activities occur) and on Indian reservations. It also acts as the main regulator for the two states (Tennessee and Washington) without a state mining authority.

Other pollution generated by mining is typically managed through state regulatory regimes, and through the federal statutes that address the media of pollution. One significant issue is the wastewater discharges from mine drainage and storm water runoff, which can significantly contaminate nearby waterways. Active mining operations are considered point sources under the Clean Water Act and are regulated under the NPDES permit scheme.[39] Abandoned mining operations, however, are treated as nonpoint source water pollution; regulating discharges from such sites is therefore left largely to the states.

TAKEAWAYS

✓ Soil pollution policy is complicated by the fact that soil pollution accumulates from a variety of sources (including both human and naturally occurring sources); the high costs of remediation; and its complex and interactive relationship with other forms of pollution.

✓ There is no single authority or legal structure tasked with managing soil pollution in the United States.

✓ Agricultural soil pollution is managed through a patchwork of non-soil-specific pollution schemes.

✓ Highly contaminated sites are identified and remediated by the federal EPA through CERCLA. Cleanup is funded partially through a "Superfund," and partially by making potentially responsible parties (including current owners) liable for cleanup costs.

✓ Soil contamination from mining activities is controlled by a cooperative federalism regime under the Surface Mining Control and Reclamation Act. This statute gives primary authority to the federal OSMRE, but allows states to regulate mining activities themselves if they can show that they meet or exceed the minimum standards of SMCRA.

DISCUSSION QUESTIONS

1. Who should pay for cleaning up contaminated sites when the party responsible for the original contamination is missing or bankrupt? Is it fair to make current owners or past owners who had nothing to do with the contamination pay for cleanup? If taxpayers pay for cleanup instead, does that create an unfair windfall for current owners?

2. How much power should states have over mining activities? Is it appropriate for the federal government to allow mining on public lands?

TOXIC SUBSTANCES
DEFINITION

Toxic substances are materials that create significant human or nonhuman environmental harm, often even when used as intended. Because these substances offer some benefits—as with pesticides, adhesives, or solvents—they are often created purposefully, rather than as a waste byproduct of other processes.

DISTINCTIVE CHALLENGES OF REGULATING TOXIC SUBSTANCES

Because toxic substances—sometimes called chemicals—are purposefully generated, regulating them requires careful consideration both of the positive expected use of the substance and its possible negative environmental impacts. As a consequence, management of toxic substances often involves complex and fact-specific balancing, which in turn often requires some method for identifying and comparing the benefits of use with the risks of exposure to the substance. Such comparisons are further complicated when substances are new, and where information about their likely impacts is scarce or uncertain.

As with waste products, the regulation of toxic substances requires an understanding of complex and often interactive processes. Different substances can combine to create increased (or decreased) harm. Moreover, chemicals can be accumulative and highly persistent, which can both delay and compound their observable harmful effects over time. Although toxic substances are generally defined by reference to their toxicity for humans, they can also have important impacts on the non-human environment.

Regulation of toxic substances implicates heightened stakes for regulators and can generate emergency conditions—for example, when there are sudden releases of toxics such as chemical spills and similar accidents. At the same time, many toxic substances play an important role in economically important production, making their regulation an economic, as well as environmental and health, concern.

KEY U.S. LEGAL APPROACHES TO TOXIC SUBSTANCES

Toxic Substances Control Act

The most significant U.S. regime for managing toxic substances is the Toxic Substances Control Act of 1976 (TSCA). In 2016, in response to what was widely perceived as a failure of TSCA to adequately protect against the harmful effects of toxic substances, Congress passed substantial amendments to the Act through the Frank R. Lautenberg Chemical Safety for the 21st Century Act.

TSCA was, and continues to be, administered by the federal EPA, which maintains an inventory list of every "chemical substance" manufactured in the United States (currently over eighty thousand substances). The Act excludes pesticides, food and drugs, and nuclear material, all of which are regulated under other specific statutes. Under the pre-2016 regime, the Act had been only rarely invoked. Tens of thousands of existing substances were grandfathered in, and while EPA was theoretically charged with performing cost-benefit analyses to address other substances, the informational burden attached to evaluating the likely costs and benefits of toxic substances proved to be largely paralyzing for the agency, which was not given many information-gathering powers in the statute. As a result, the EPA successfully banned only five substances in the first forty years of the TSCA.[40]

The Lautenberg Act responded to these challenges in three significant ways. First, it changed the calculation that the EPA makes to decide which substances to regulate by shifting the TSCA's focus from a cost-benefit analysis approach to a system that centers on determining the "conditions of use" of regulated substances through risk analysis. These "conditions of use" focus on how the substance is used, and how people are exposed to it, rather than focusing exclusively on the potential hazardous properties of the substance in isolation from its use, or on cost considerations. Second, the EPA must now also consider the safety of existing substances, which were previously grandfathered in, not only new substances. To fulfill this responsibility, it must have at least twenty chemical risk evaluations ongoing at any time. Third, the statute empowers the EPA to order the development of new information when knowledge about a substance's impacts is too limited for an educated decision regarding regulation.

In sum, in regulating toxic substances, the United States has moved away from its prior dependence on cost-benefit analysis, instead doubling down on risk analysis as a basis for the regulation of toxic substances. This can largely be explained by the complex informational burden required to understand the likely impacts of those substances. The current method of risk analysis attempts to weigh the beneficial uses of toxics against their safety, as determined by their conditions of use, and to incentivize the creation of additional information to limit uncertainty.

Pesticide Regulation: FIFRA

Pesticides—including insecticides, fungicides, and rodenticides—are regulated by the Federal Insecticide, Fungicide, and Rodenticide Act (FIFRA), which requires that all pesticides distributed or sold in the United States be registered with the EPA. Before a pesticide can be registered, the applicant must show that using the pesticide as directed "will not generally cause unreasonable adverse effects on the environment," meaning "any unreasonable risk to man or the environment, taking into account the economic, social, and environmental costs and benefits of the use of any pesticide." To determine whether a substance meets this standard, the EPA typically performs a quantified cost-benefit analysis using risk analysis techniques, explicitly balancing the beneficial uses of the pesticide with its expected harms. Thus, for the particular category of toxic substances used as pesticides, the United States retains a significant dependence on cost-benefit analysis, with risk analysis providing the methods for gathering information and assessing risk and uncertainty.

Toxic Disclosure Regimes

Toxic disclosure regimes help manage exposure to toxic substances by disclosing the presence or emission of a toxic substance, so that members of the public can reduce their exposure by changing their behaviors.

The Emergency Planning and Community Right-to-Know Act (EPCRA) provides the federal legal regime for managing emergency releases of toxic substances. The Act was passed in response to the tragic Bhopal disaster in India, where a chemical plant leaked deadly methyl isocyanate gas into the surrounding environment, killing thousands immediately—many in their sleep—and many thousands more from long-term effects of exposure. EPCRA was designed to address the possibility of sudden toxic emissions by creating a system of public notification and emergency response.

To serve this end, EPCRA created three primary mechanisms: state-based requirements for emergency response planning; industry reporting requirements on hazardous chemical inventories that might be the source of future releases; and notification of chemical accidents and releases. The best-known feature of EPCRA is the Toxics Release Inventory (TRI), which requires facilities of a certain size to report all releases of listed toxic pollutants. The reports must be made annually using a standardized form provided by the EPA, which makes them available through an internet database searchable by location and facility name.[41] Currently, more than six hundred chemicals are covered by the TRI, a number that continues to grow in response to citizen petitions and occasional legislative action. The decision of whether and when to list a substance remains controversial, however, and lawsuits often result from the EPA's decision to add (or refuse to add) a substance to the TRI.

The United States also has a number of labeling-based disclosure requirements, intended to warn of potential exposure to toxic substances in products. One of these is the Federal Hazardous Substances Act (FHSA), administered by the Consumer Product Safety Commission. The FHSA requires precautionary labeling on the container of all hazardous household products to help consumers safely store and use those products and to give them information about immediate first aid steps to take if an accident happens. As discussed above, there is also the well-known Proposition 65 label, which requires warnings on products known to the State of California to cause cancer or reproductive harm.

Toxic Torts and Common Law Liability

Alongside the statutory and regulatory regimes created for regulating toxic substances, the United States maintains a robust common law system for addressing harms from toxic substances through tort law. The U.S. Supreme Court has held that suits for damages from toxic substances are not precluded by the existence of, or compliance with, toxics statutory regimes. This means that those who can show they were harmed by a substance can sue in court for damages and sometimes for injunctions, regardless of the statutory regime. These suits tend to be based on state law in tort regarding product liability and negligence. In some large cases, suits for so-called "toxic torts" have resulted in damage awards exceeding a billion dollars.[42] Such suits provide a mechanism for addressing distributional harm, and the potential for liability can also provide a disincentive for companies to allow toxic exposures.

TAKEAWAYS

✓ Toxic substances present distinctive challenges to regulation because they are purposefully created, meaning that it is often necessary to do fact-specific balancing between beneficial uses and potential environmental impact.

✓ The U.S. approach to many toxic substances has shifted away from a pure cost-benefit approach to a balancing requirement that focuses on the risks attached to substances under their intended conditions of use. The United States continues to rely on risk analysis to assess the risks of toxic substances, but it now affirmatively requires the creation of new information regarding poorly understood substances.

✓ Pesticides are regulated under their own statutory regime, which is based on cost-benefit balancing of the dangers and benefits of various pesticides.

✓ The United States has a variety of federal and state toxics disclosure regimes that attempt to manage the risks of toxics by providing information about exposure, which may help people reduce their risk by changing their behaviors.

✓ Common law liability remains an important backstop for the regulation of toxic substances in the United States.

DISCUSSION QUESTIONS

1. How should society weigh the usefulness of substances against their toxicity? What should be done when the toxicity of a substance is unknown—is it better to err on the side of limiting the use of useful but potentially dangerous substances, or to allow useful substances to be used unless it is clear they are also unreasonably harmful?

2. Does it make sense to have prospective regulation of toxic substances *and* the possibility of retrospective judicial liability when people are exposed to toxic substances? Why not rely entirely on prospective regulation or entirely on the possibility of liability?

WASTE MANAGEMENT

DEFINITION

Waste is a material or substance that is discarded as no longer useful. Waste can be classified as solid waste (nonhazardous waste in solid, as opposed to liquid or gaseous, form), hazardous waste (waste with properties that make it dangerous to human health or the environment), or nuclear waste (waste from nuclear reactions, including spent nuclear fuel).

DISTINCTIVE CHALLENGES OF MANAGING WASTE

Particular types of waste (table 6) can implicate specific challenges, depending on the behaviors that create the waste and the risks posed by

TABLE 6

Types of Waste

Type	Definition	Key Source(s)	Example
Solid	Nonhazardous discarded materials	Individuals, municipalities, and industry	Garbage
Hazardous	Wastes with properties that make them dangerous or potentially harmful to human health or the environment	Concentrated industrial processes	Chemical waste
Radioactive	Waste that emits substantial radiation	Military and/or nuclear energy production	Spent nuclear fuel

waste transport, storage, and disposal. Moreover, waste management implicates substantial interactions with other forms of pollution control, in that poorly managed waste can lead to water pollution or soil pollution, incineration of waste can cause air pollution, and the production of toxic substances can create waste.

Municipal solid waste—trash or garbage—consists of everyday items that are used and then discarded, including product packaging, food scraps, and paper products. Because generation of trash is extraordinarily diffuse, a significant aspect of trash management involves transportation activities designed to concentrate the waste for recycling and disposal.

Hazardous waste, by contrast, is often the result of concentrated industrial processes, which offers opportunities for direct regulation at the industrial plants. That said, some consumer behaviors—such as disposal of batteries or paint cans—can also generate hazardous waste; these behaviors often present additional challenges in regulating. The hazards of the underlying material also create special risks in its transportation, storage, and disposal, and many hazardous wastes present long-term risks to humans and ecosystems if handled inappropriately.

Like hazardous waste, the generation of nuclear waste tends to be highly concentrated. The special hazards of nuclear waste heighten issues surrounding transportation, storage, and disposal. In addition, nuclear waste implicates distinctive challenges because of long time horizons: nuclear waste takes many hundreds of thousands of years to decay, creating significant uncertainty in predicting long-term effects and likelihood of leakage.

A challenge of all types of waste is that waste disposal tends to concentrate an undesirable environmental impact in one location. As a result, waste disposal often implicates local protectionism—sometimes referred to as the "Not in my backyard," or NIMBY, phenomenon. This can also create distributional challenges in determining where—and next to whom—waste services are sited. One concern is that undesirable land that can be used for waste disposal tends to be located near disadvantaged communities (particularly African American and Hispanic communities). NIMBY concerns are also especially prevalent for nuclear waste disposal. Although the United States has long sought to develop a centralized nuclear waste depository in Yucca Mountain, Nevada, political constraints have meant that no such depository is operating or likely to come into existence soon. As a result, nuclear waste continues to be stored at decentralized sites across the United States, typically at or near one of the sixty-one commercially operating nuclear power plants, which are spread over thirty states.

Finally, unlike many other forms of pollution, the management of waste gives rise to a significant industry. In fact, the United States is the world's largest market for solid and hazardous waste services.[43] Solid waste disposal alone is a $97 billion industry, and best estimates suggest that waste management is responsible for about one two-hundredth of the U.S. Gross Domestic Product and contributes over nine hundred thousand jobs to the U.S. economy.[44]

KEY U.S. LEGAL APPROACHES
TO WASTE MANAGEMENT

The most important federal law addressing waste management is the Resource Conservation and Recovery Act of 1976 (RCRA), which identifies separate frameworks for dealing with nonhazardous and hazardous wastes. Nuclear and radioactive waste is managed primarily through the Nuclear Waste Policy Act of 1982 (NWPA).

Solid Waste: State Management and Deposit-Refund Systems

Under RCRA, solid wastes are defined as any "garbage, refuse, sludge from a waste treatment plant, water supply treatment plant, or air pollution control facility and other discarded material, including solid, liquid, semisolid, or contained gaseous material resulting from industrial, commercial, mining, and agricultural operations." The statute distinguishes sharply between hazardous and nonhazardous solid wastes. Hazardous wastes, which pose special risks to human health, are regulated under Subtitle C of the Act (and are discussed further in the next subsection). Nonhazardous solid wastes are regulated under Subtitle D and do not have to comply with the stringent requirements of Subtitle C.[45]

For nonhazardous solid wastes, RCRA encourages states to take a primary role, by requiring them to develop comprehensive plans for managing nonhazardous solid waste. The Act also sets minimum criteria for solid waste disposal facilities, and prohibits open dumping of solid waste.

The United States generates about 250 million tons of nonhazardous solid waste a year, or about 4.4 pounds (2 kg) per person per day. Landfills remain the primary method of municipal solid waste disposal, and there are approximately two thousand municipal waste landfills (a significant decrease from over six thousand landfills in 1990). In some cases, densely populated states such as New York ship trash to landfills out of state.

On average, the United States recycles 35 percent of all municipal waste. State schemes and rates for recycling management vary. Ten states have so-called "container deposit" legislation—consumers pay a deposit (which varies from five to ten cents per container) that they receive back upon returning the container for recycling. These states achieve an average of 70 percent recycling on items included in the deposit-refund system.

Plastic waste presents a special case. Until 2018, when China changed its plastic import policies, the United States shipped the majority of its plastic waste to China for recycling. In the absence of federal policy on plastics recycling, states and municipalities continue to scramble to find methods for managing plastic waste.[46]

Hazardous Waste: Cradle-to-Grave Tracking and TSDFs

As mentioned above, RCRA includes a separate set of provisions—Subtitle C—dealing specifically with the heightened risks posed by hazardous waste. To manage these risks, RCRA was designed to establish a "cradle to grave" system for regulating hazardous waste; as a result, such waste is regulated from the time it is created, through transportation, treatment, and storage, until disposal. The resulting regime accordingly includes specific regulatory requirements for each stage of the waste's life cycle.

The classification of waste as "hazardous" is complicated and remains contentious within RCRA.[47] As a general matter, generators of waste are responsible for making an initial determination as to whether their waste is hazardous and must oversee waste disposal. Generators are also required to document waste production, treatment, and recycling or disposal. Producers of significant quantities of hazardous waste are subject to additional requirements under RCRA. The Act also distinguishes Treatment Storage and Disposal Facilities (TSDFs), which provide temporary storage and final treatment or disposal for hazardous wastes. Because these facilities may present a higher degree of risk over time, RCRA establishes relatively expansive requirements for their management, including significant procedural and reporting requirements.

While RCRA plays a central role in helping to regulate hazardous waste and prevent spills, once hazardous waste contaminates a site, management of cleanup and remediation are primarily addressed under CERCLA.[48]

Nuclear Waste: The Nuclear Waste Policy Act and Yucca Mountain

Nuclear waste is managed under NWPA, which aimed to establish a permanent, underground repository for high-level radioactive waste by the mid-1990s. This facility was to provide a safe place for the very long-term storage of both civilian nuclear waste (including over sixty thousand metric tons of spent fuel from civilian power plants) and of some military-created waste (such as that created as a byproduct of building nuclear weapons).

Congress tasked the newly created Office of Civilian Radioactive Waste Management within the Department of Energy with implementing the Act. In 1987, Congress amended the Act to designate the remotely located Yucca Mountain, Nevada, as the sole disposal site for high-level radioactive waste. The NWPA allowed a state to veto placement of a nuclear waste depository within its borders, with the veto to be overruled only by a vote of both houses of Congress. In an illustration of "NIMBY" challenges facing nuclear waste storage, Nevada did veto placement of the Yucca Mountain repository within its borders; this was then overruled by both houses of Congress. However, in 2010,

President Barack Obama rejected use of the site and zeroed out funding for nuclear waste disposal. The ultimate fate of Yucca Mountain and of centralized nuclear waste storage thus remains uncertain.

Without a central repository, nuclear waste in the United States is stored at or near one of the 121 facilities where it is generated. The NWPA allows for two storage methods for spent fuel after it is removed from a reactor core: it may be stored in spent fuel pools, which are specially designed pools at individual reactor sites (typically made of reinforced concrete several feet thick, with steel liners, and water about forty feet deep); or it may be stored in dry cask storage, which is typically used when spent fuel pools become full. Over sixty thousand metric tons of commercial radioactive spent fuel is stored in the United States; of this, about 75 percent is stored in pools and 25 percent in casks. With pools now largely full, and with no central repository to send accumulated waste, the proportion of spent fuel stored in casks is expected to grow in coming years.

TAKEAWAYS

✓ Regulation of waste requires involvement with the substantial waste management industry and is complicated by the fact that concentrating waste tends to create undesirable land uses, which then interact with other forms of pollution. In addition, municipal solid waste presents challenges from the diffusion of its creation; control of hazardous is complicated by the hazards of the underlying material; and nuclear waste has to be managed over extraordinarily long time horizons.

✓ In the United States, waste is managed differently depending on whether it is categorized as solid waste, hazardous waste, or nuclear waste. Each of these categories is regulated under a different statutory regime and, in the case of nuclear waste, a different agency.

✓ Solid waste is primarily managed by the states. This includes management of municipal solid waste, the majority of which goes to landfills, and of recycling. Some states operate deposit-refund systems to encourage container recycling; recycling rates in those states are double the national average.

✓ Hazardous waste is regulated under the federal Resource Conservation and Recovery Act, which creates a set of regulations that apply to hazardous waste generators and to transporters, storers, and disposal facilities.

✓ Nuclear waste storage remains decentralized despite many political attempts to concentrate disposal.

DISCUSSION QUESTIONS

1. How centralized should waste management policies be? Does the answer depend on the type of waste being managed—solid waste, hazardous waste, or nuclear waste?

2. Do you object to states or countries shipping their waste elsewhere? What incentives does shipping waste create for the producers of products, and for users of those products?

3. Waste management sites, such as landfills, are locally undesirable, even though they serve a valuable social function. How and where should they be sited?

POLLUTION CONTROL: SUMMARY

The U.S. approach to pollution control varies according to the type of pollution addressed. In general, however, U.S. pollution control law is characterized by a cooperative federalist structure, in which the federal government works to coordinate implementation with states. Administrative agencies play an important role in administering U.S. pollution control, with the EPA administering most of the major pollution control statutes. Risk analysis and cost-benefit analysis inform agency policy, and otherwise play varying roles in various pollution control regimes.

KEY TERMS

AIR POLLUTION Higher-than-normal concentrations of materials, including chemicals, that are out of place in air.

COOPERATIVE FEDERALISM System of cooperation between federal and state governments, commonly used in the implementation of U.S. pollution control statutes.

CRITERIA POLLUTANTS Common air pollutants for which the Environmental Protection Agency sets National Ambient Air Quality Standards under the Clean Air Act.

DOSE-RESPONSE Relationship between the amount of a substance an organism is exposed to and the harm and response the exposure causes.

EXPOSURE REDUCTION Amending behavior so that there is less exposure to pollution and, thus (hopefully) less harm.

NATIONAL AMBIENT AIR QUALITY STANDARDS (NAAQS) Health-based standards set under the Clean Air Act for the quantity of criteria pollutants that may be in the air.

NUISANCE An act that is unreasonably harmful to the public (public nuisance) or to an individual (private nuisance) and for which there is a judicial remedy.

SOIL POLLUTION Higher-than-normal concentrations of materials, including chemicals, that are out of place in soil.

SOURCE REDUCTION Amending behavior to reduce the amount of pollution initially created (at the "source").

TORT A civil (as opposed to criminal) wrong that creates a cause of action for suing in court.

TOXIC SUBSTANCES Materials, sometimes referred to as "chemicals," that create significant human or nonhuman environmental harm, even when used as intended.

WASTE A material, substance, or byproduct that is discarded as no longer useful.

WATER POLLUTION Higher-than-normal concentrations of materials, including chemicals, that are out of place in water, including drinking water.

DISCUSSION QUESTIONS

1. Which type of pollution is most important, or are they all equally important? Why do we care about pollutants at all?

2. How can regulators know when they have created a successful pollution control regime?

3. Should regulators seek to eliminate all pollution? If not, how should they determine how much pollution is tolerable?

NOTES

1. One early public-nuisance pollution case—*Missouri v. Illinois,* 200 U.S. 496 (1906)—illustrates some of the challenges inherent in the common law approach. In that case, the State of Missouri sued the State of Illinois for dumping sewage and meatpacking waste into a river that flowed into the Mississippi River, which many cities and towns in Missouri relied on for drinking and agriculture. A number of Missouri residents sickened, and some died of typhoid. Ultimately, Missouri was unable to establish a clear enough causal

connection between Illinois' polluting behavior and the harm Missouri was bearing, and the case was dismissed.

2. For a useful list of state environmental agencies, see www.epa.gov /home/health-and-environmental-agencies-us-states-and-territories.

3. Greenhouse gas emissions are a type of air pollution that contributes to climate disruption. They are addressed in more detail in chapter 8.

4. See EPA, BENEFITS AND COSTS OF THE CLEAN AIR ACT 1990–2020, the Second Prospective Study, www.epa.gov/clean-air-act-overview/benefits-and-costs-clean-air-act.

5. For this comparison, as well as a technical overview of the Clean Air Act, see Richard Revesz et al., Environmental Law and Policy (4th ed., Foundation Press 2019).

6. See www.epa.gov/environmental-topics/air-topics, including a very helpful and readable overview in THE PLAIN ENGLISH GUIDE TO THE CLEAN AIR ACT, www.epa.gov/sites/production/files/2015-08/documents/peg.pdf. The Revesz volume noted above also provides valuable discussion directed toward advanced U.S. law students.

7. See EPA, BENEFITS AND COSTS OF THE CLEAN AIR ACT 1990–2020, THE SECOND PROSPECTIVE STUDY, www.epa.gov/clean-air-act-overview/benefits-and-costs-clean-air-act.

8. The Supreme Court case on point is *Whitman v. American Trucking Associations, Inc.*, 531 U.S. 457 (2001).

9. This is discussed in more detail in chapter 8.

10. Also called particle pollution, particulate matter is made up of tiny suspended solids and liquid droplets of various materials. Some of these—such as soot, smoke, or dust—can be large enough to see with the naked eye; others are so small they can only be detected with a powerful microscope. Under the NAAQS, the EPA sets two particulate matter standards, one for finer and more dangerous particles ($PM_{2.5}$) and one for larger and relatively less dangerous particles (PM_{10}).

11. See www.epa.gov/clean-air-act-overview/progress-cleaning-air-and-improving-peoples-health.

12. See www.epa.gov/green-book.

13. See www.airnow.gov.

14. See www3.epa.gov/airquality/greenbook/mapnpoll.html.

15. Although California has only 12 percent of the U.S. population, much of the state is covered in mountainous terrain that traps pollution over population centers, and its warm climate contributes to the creation of ozone and other criteria air pollutants.

16. For a discussion of grandfathering in the Clean Air Act, see Jonathan Remy Nash and Richard Revesz, *Grandfathering and Environmental Regulation: The Law and Economics of New Source Review,* 101 Nw. U. L. Rev. 1677 (2007).

17. EPA, NATIONAL EMISSION STANDARDS FOR HAZARDOUS AIR POLLUTANTS, www.epa.gov/stationary-sources-air-pollution/national-emission-standards-hazardous-air-pollutants-neshap-9.

18. 206 U.S. 230 (1907).

19. Alan Barreca, Matthew Neidell, and Nicholas Sanders, *Long-Run Pollution Exposure and Adult Mortality: Evidence from the Acid Rain Program,* National Bureau of Economic Research (June 2017), www.nber.org/papers /w23524.pdf.

20. The Cross-State Air Pollution Rule has had a complicated history, and continues to be reviewed by courts. EPA maintains an updated resource on the rule at www.epa.gov/csapr.

21. The EPA maintains a list of other international cooperation programs for air pollution at www.epa.gov/international-cooperation/transboundary-air-pollution.

22. See *Madison v. Ducktown Sulphur, Copper & Iron Co.,* 113 Tenn. 331 (1904).

23. See *Georgia v. Tennessee Copper Co.,* 206 U.S. 230 (1907).

24. See *AEP v. Connecticut,* 564 U.S. 410 (2011); see also *Bell v. Cheswick Generating Station* (3d Cir. 2013).

25. See Trail Smelter Arbitration, U.S.-Canada, Trail Smelter Arbitral Tribunal (August 16, 1938). For analysis of the central importance of the Trail Smelter decision within international environmental law, see Rebecca Bratspies and Russell Miller (eds.), TRANSBOUNDARY HARM IN INTERNATIONAL LAW: LESSONS FROM THE TRAIL SMELTER ARBITRATION (Cambridge University Press 2010).

26. The CWA is sometimes also referred to as the "Federal Water Pollution Control Act."

27. Some (though not all) states have chosen to develop their own standards for groundwater and stream flow, and water quantity issues remain largely managed through state law.

28. See Clean Water Act, § 101(a). The EPA maintains a summary of various portions of the Clean Water Act, as well as information on compliance and enforcement, at www.epa.gov/laws-regulations/summary-clean-water-act.

29. The EPA maintains a set of resources on nonpoint source water pollution at www.epa.gov/nps/basic-information-about-nonpoint-source-nps-pollution.

30. The EPA keeps an updated database of state information on water quality at https://ofmpub.epa.gov/waters10/attains_nation_cy.control#total_assessed_waters.

31. For a recent thoughtful evaluation of the effects of the Clean Water Act, see David A. Keiser and Joseph Shapiro, *Consequences of the Clean Water Act and the Demand for Water Quality,* 134 Q.J. ECONOMICS 349 (2019).

32. See *Rapanos v. United States,* 547 U.S. 715 (2006). For further discussion, see spotlight 16, "Waters of the United States."

33. For a discussion of the complexities of coastal water quality protection by one of the foremost experts in U.S. water law, see Robin Kundis Craig, *Coastal Water Quality Protection,* in Donald Baur, Tim Eichenberg, and Michael Sutton (eds.), OCEAN & COASTAL L. & POL'Y 235–274 (American Bar Association 2015). For a treatment of law relating to ocean acidification, and the challenges faced by nonpoint source regulation, see Robin Kundis Craig, *Dealing with Ocean Acidification: The Problem, the Clean Water Act, and State and Regional Approaches,* 6 WASH. J. ENVTL. L. & POL'Y 387 (2016).

34. The database can be accessed online at https://watersgeo.epa.gov /beacon2/.

35. For a list of laws and regulations that apply to agricultural activities, including those that may cause soil contamination, see www.epa.gov/agriculture /agriculture-laws-and-regulations-apply-your-agricultural-operation-farm-activity.

36. See www.epa.gov/superfund/search-superfund-sites-where-you-live, which lists all Superfund sites. Delaware has the greatest concentration.

37. For a discussion of the controversial and expansive scope of CERCLA liability, see Owen Smith, *The Expansive Scope of Liable Parties under CERCLA,* 63 ST. JOHN'S L. REV. 821 (2012), http://scholarship.law.stjohns.edu/cgi/viewcontent .cgi?article = 1956&context = lawreview.

38. See www.eia.gov/coal/annual/pdf/table1.pdf.

39. The EPA has issued specific regulations to address mining impacts on water pollution. See Mineral Mining and Processing Effluent Guidelines and Standards, 40 CFR Part 736.

40. The EPA was famously prevented from banning asbestos in the case *Corrosion Proof Fittings v. EPA,* 947 F.2d 1201 (5th Cir. 1991).

41. The EPA maintains this database and related resources on its website at www.epa.gov/toxics-release-inventory-tri-program.

42. Very large damage awards are not always upheld by courts. In one 2019 case, for example, a California jury awarded over two billion dollars to a husband and wife who alleged that they had each developed cancer as a result of decades of exposure to Monsanto's weed killer Roundup. The judge subsequently reduced the damage award to $86 million.

43. See United States International Trade Commission, Solid and Hazardous Waste Services: An Examination of U.S. and Foreign Markets (2004), www.usitc.gov/publications/332/pub3679.pdf.

44. Environmental Research and Education Foundation, Size of the U.S. Solid Waste Industry (2001), https://erefdn.org/wp-content/uploads/2015/12/SizeoftheSolidWasteIndusty.pdf.

45. Because the regulatory requirements for nonhazardous and hazardous solid waste differ so significantly, notable effort is often invested in distinguishing between the types of waste. The EPA maintains a resource for distinguishing which requirements apply at www.epa.gov/hw/criteria-definition-solid-waste-and-solid-and-hazardous-waste-exclusions.

46. For a quick overview of the challenges the United States faces in plastic recycling, see Christopher Joyce, Where Will Your Plastic Trash Go Now That China Doesn't Want It?, National Public Radio (March 13, 2019).

47. The EPA maintains a set of resources for categorizing and addressing hazardous waste, available at www.epa.gov/hw.

48. For treatment of CERCLA, see the snapshot on "Soil Pollution."

CHAPTER SEVEN

Ecosystem Management

This chapter sets out the essentials of the U.S. legal approach to ecosystem management. It begins by defining the general problems presented by ecosystem management. It then describes the fundamentals of the U.S. approach to these problems, before providing snapshots of the strategies on which the United States relies for five important types of ecosystem management: (1) protecting and promoting general biodiversity; (2) protecting, managing, and restoring particular wildlife, including endangered species; (3) protecting and managing special types of ecosystems, such as wetlands; (4) protecting and managing particular areas, as with the creation of National Parks and Marine Reserves, and the management of public lands; and (5) managing agriculture and food production.

ECOSYSTEM MANAGEMENT AS AN ENVIRONMENTAL PROBLEM

Ecological systems, or *ecosystems,* are geographic areas where living entities (plants, animals, and other organisms) and nonliving entities (including water, air, and soil) interact in mutually interdependent ways. Ecosystem management seeks to preserve, sustain, and secure whole ecosystems and the qualities of ecosystems that are deemed valuable.

Since humans evolved, human activities have affected ecosystems. When performed deliberately, however, ecosystem management requires policymakers to trade off competing social, cultural, and environmental values, as when they must balance the destruction of a biodiverse wetland against the social benefits of development. In managing the ecosystems under their control, policymakers may choose to allow, prevent, or mitigate ecosystem degradation, which occurs whenever valued aspects of an ecosystem are harmed. Policymakers may also attempt to repair past degradation through ecosystem restoration, or to purposefully change existing ecosystems to secure more of whatever is valued.

To accurately predict the impacts of policy choices on ecosystems, policymakers depend on information about how living and nonliving entities relate to and depend on one another, through time as well as over space. As discussed in chapter 1, the impacts of human action on the nonhuman environment are typically diffuse and complex, implicating a series of natural and scientific processes that can be difficult to detect, predict, and understand. Where ecological systems are involved, these impacts may be particularly interactive, so that a small change in input may create substantial environmental consequences within that ecosystem and within related ecosystems. Management of these impacts is made all the more complicated by scientific research suggesting both that many ecosystems exhibit some level of resilience to disruption and that there may also be nonlinear "tipping points" where even small changes may destroy whole ecosystems. To prevent unintentional and potentially irreversible consequences, ecosystem management systems must incorporate some method for collecting and processing information about the nonhuman environment, and about the likely impacts of human (in)action. In many cases, however, that information is likely to be incomplete, and impacts may remain uncertain or change rapidly.

Even where ecosystem managers can call upon high-quality scientific information, they still face substantial policy challenges. These include defining the geographic and temporal spaces that should be protected; coordinating ecosystem management with other environmental policies; and, most controversially, determining which qualities of ecosystems are valuable enough to justify policy intervention.

One set of important policy decisions is related to the appropriate scope of ecosystem management. How far into the future should ecosystems be protected, and when ecosystems are being restored, to what point in time should they be restored? While many countries have adopted rhetoric about maintaining "sustainable ecosystems," commentators increasingly warn that the term *sustainability* can be misleading in obscuring value-laden decisions about the time frame of concern, the benefits and costs that matter, and the relative priority of economic, social, and environmental benefits and costs over time.[1] Attempts to manage ecosystems are further complicated by the fact that plants, animals, and other organisms may develop biological and environmental interdependencies with adjacent ecosystems, or even with plants, animals, and organisms that are geographically distant. The difficulty of defining ecosystems geographically leads to substantial tension in determining what level of government (local, state, federal, international) is best suited to manage any particular ecosystem.

The regulatory complexity of ecosystem management is not limited to managing multiple levels of government. The interaction between ecosystem management and other environmental regimes—including legal mechanisms for managing the sources of potential harm to ecosystems, such as pollution policy or natural resource use—adds a further layer of complexity. These policies may or may not address specific ecosystems (such as wetlands) or specific qualities of ecosystems (such as biodiversity), but they may nevertheless have a substantial impact on ecosystems. For example, schemes for managing aquatic ecosystems must often account for risks of acid rain, a potentially devastating source of aquatic ecosystem degradation, which increases the acidity of rivers, lakes, and aquatic environments and leads to toxic leaching of soil-based aluminum. Acid rain risk, however, is primarily driven by emissions of sulfur dioxide and nitrogen oxides, gases that are typically regulated through air pollution regimes.

Finally, goal setting for ecosystem management is inherently controversial because different peoples and groups hold clashing views about which qualities of an ecosystem should be promoted, to what extent, and why. On this front, consider that one influential way to evaluate the value of ecosystems is to focus on which benefits they provide to humans. These "ecosystem services"[2] range from providing food and water, to regulating climate and flood risk, to providing cultural and recreational opportunities.[3] While the identification of ecosystem services can be helpful for policymakers, it also raises the important (and controversial) question of whether ecosystems are valuable solely because of their "services"—that is, for how they harm or benefit humans—or whether ecosystems should also be managed to protect nonhuman plants, animals, or organisms for their own sake, regardless of their benefit to humans.[4]

Legal systems have developed different answers to the question of when—if ever—the law ought to protect nonhuman interests. In most jurisdictions, environmental law remains focused—sometimes exclusively—on shaping the environment for the benefit of humans. Yet there are a number of exceptions to this general rule. In New Zealand, for example, the Whanganui River ecosystem has been recognized as a legal entity with the same rights, duties, and liabilities as any legal person. And even in jurisdictions like the United States, where most environmental law is focused exclusively on human interests, a few exceptions arguably apply. In the United States, the most significant example of apparent incorporation of nonhuman interests into environmental policy is the treatment of endangered species—notably, the Endangered Species Act protects the habitats of (some) endangered animal species, even where those species present no quantifiable benefit to humans.

KEY CHARACTERISTICS OF U.S. ECOSYSTEM
MANAGEMENT

The United States is home to an incredibly diverse set of ecosystems, some of which are unique in the world. The services provided by these ecosystems are used heavily by humans—for recreation, habitation, agriculture, and extraction of timber, water, and other resources. The use of these systems almost inevitably leads to a certain amount of degradation.

In the United States, ecosystems are managed by a variety of federal, state, local, and private actors, all of whom make decisions that can impact ecosystems and ecosystem degradation. Because ecosystems are tied to geographic space, land use law and property law play an important role in ecosystem management. Most land use and property law regimes in the United States are governed by states, which often delegate substantial responsibility to local and municipal governments. Zoning and land use decisions, in particular, may substantially impact local ecosystems, and these decisions are generally managed by local and municipal zoning boards, administrative bodies that decide the location and type of construction, development, and use that will be locally permitted. Because the jurisdictions of zoning boards and local municipalities do not necessarily match up with the natural and ecological borders of ecosystems, this often creates a patchwork system of regulation, which can lead to community action problems where a larger ecosystem is spread across multiple jurisdictions.

Although states retain significant power to manage local ecosystems, federal law also plays an important role in many aspects of ecosystem management. Other than the Property Clause, which provides the constitutional basis for the federal government's direct administration of more than a quarter of U.S. land, the U.S. Constitution is silent on the subject of ecosystem management. That said, in addition to federal pollution control schemes that often affect ecosystem quality, a number of federal statutes articulate particular and sometimes quite powerful ways that the federal government manages and controls ecosystems, either directly or through the management of the services they provide (table 7). Particularly notably, in addition to statutes directing the management of public lands, federal statutes also govern the treatment of endangered species and the management of special types of ecosystems (particularly wetlands). These statutes are administered by federal agencies, whose interpretations of the statutes are subject to review by U.S. courts.

In addition, the National Environmental Protection Act of 1969 (NEPA) plays a critical informational role in requiring federal actions to undergo environmental assessment, and in generating information needed to understand the impacts of significant government actions on complex ecosystems. NEPA often plays a companion role with other statutes and legal requirements; for example, environmental assessments required by NEPA are often how agencies realize that their actions may affect endangered species, which then triggers the substantial protections of the Endangered Species Act.

TABLE 7

Important Federal Statutes Affecting Ecosystem Management

Statute	Target
National Environmental Policy Act	Requires federal agencies to assess the environmental effects of their proposed actions prior to making decisions
Endangered Species Act	Protects endangered and threatened species of animals and plants from public and private actions
Clean Water Act	Generally promotes water quality, and specifically protects and restores wetlands (§404)
National Park Service Act	Creates a system of creating, protecting, and conserving National Parks
Federal Land Policy and Management Act	Articulates the national policy for managing public lands

DISCUSSION QUESTIONS

1. Who benefits from good ecosystem management, and who suffers from poor ecosystem management?

2. How should policymakers balance the economic value of ecosystems with their environmental value? Should policymakers treat ecosystems or species as having intrinsic value, separate from their value to humans? If so, how should that affect policy?

3. How can policymakers or the public know that an ecosystem is being managed poorly? What about when an ecosystem is being managed well?

LEGAL SNAPSHOTS: ECOSYSTEM MANAGEMENT IN THE UNITED STATES

The next section provides a series of "snapshots" explaining how the United States engages in five important types of ecosystem management: (1) protecting and promoting general biodiversity; (2) protecting, managing, and restoring particular forms of wildlife (as with measures to protect endangered species); (3) protecting, managing, and restoring special types of ecosystems (such as wetlands); (4) protecting and managing particular ecosystems (as with the creation of National Parks, and in the management of public lands); and (5) agriculture.

BIODIVERSITY
DEFINITION

Biological diversity, or *biodiversity,* represents the variety of life in a habitat or ecosystem. This may refer to diversity within species, between species, and/or among ecosystems.

DISTINCTIVE CHALLENGES OF MANAGING BIODIVERSITY

Science has described about 1.5 million species of life on Earth, though scientists estimate that the true number could be closer to ten million. Diverse species, and interactions between those species, have developed over millennia in response to vastly varying environmental, natural, and human-led processes. Biodiversity is a measure of the number and variety of these forms of life.

It is intrinsically challenging to understand the health and resilience of every variety of life in even a single habitat or ecosystem; understanding the best policies for promoting biodiversity across habitats and ecosystems is even more complex. This means that, for biodiversity policy, informational burdens loom large. Often, however, there is limited information about the long-term and systemic impacts of changing or eliminating specific forms of life.

Even where policymakers have significant information about the variety of life in an ecosystem, they still face tough policy choices about when and how much to prioritize biodiversity over competing values. One particularly common tension comes from trade-offs between biodiversity and development: much of the time, developing land for economic purposes destroys at least a portion (and sometimes all) of the variety of life living on that land.

Trade-offs like these often require policymakers to determine whether, how, and why they value biodiversity. Is biodiversity good only for the ways that it benefits humans through ecosystem services— for example, by offering the potential for lifesaving new medical treatments or (indirectly) by sustaining other life-forms within the relevant ecosystem? Is it also valuable for separate moral or ethical reasons—for example, because humans have an obligation to protect nonhuman populations or to sustain the Earth as they found it? Policymakers' answers to these difficult questions can inform whether they adopt general biodiversity policies, which seek to promote and protect the variety of life regardless of the type of life or its apparent value to humans, or whether they adopt more specific policies tailored toward preserving specific ecosystems or particular forms of life.

KEY U.S. LEGAL APPROACHES TO BIODIVERSITY

Many countries around the world have formal policies regarding the preservation and promotion of biodiversity. The United States is an outlier in this instance: it has no single, formal, national policy on biodiversity. It is also the only United Nations member state that has chosen not to join the Convention on Biological Diversity (see spotlight 15), an international treaty that opened for signature in 1992, which is aimed at ensuring the development of national biodiversity plans and the international sharing of the benefits that arise from genetic resources.[5]

(Paragraph continues on p. 161)

SPOTLIGHT 15. CONVENTION ON BIOLOGICAL DIVERSITY

The Convention on Biological Diversity, sometimes called the "Biodiversity Convention," is a multilateral agreement designed to strategize for and to promote the conservation and sustainable use of biological diversity in light of "the intrinsic value of biological diversity" and "the ecological, genetic, social, economic, scientific, educational, cultural, recreational and aesthetic values of biological diversity and its components." Around the world, the Convention is widely viewed as the key international framework promoting sustainable development.

The Convention requires parties to prepare a national biodiversity strategy, and creates a set of incentives for conservation and sustainable use, including a funding mechanism for developing countries that commit to critical biodiversity conservation projects. It has been ratified by 196 parties, including the European Union and 192 of the 193 United Nations member states. The United States has signed, but never ratified, the Convention. As a result, the United States is the only UN member state that is not a member of the treaty.

The Convention has been supplemented by two protocols that address particular issues related to biodiversity: the Cartagena Protocol on Biosafety, adopted in 2000; and the Nagoya Protocol on Access to Genetic Resources and the Fair and Equitable Sharing of Benefits Arising from their Utilization to the Convention on Biological Diversity, adopted in 2010. The United States has signed, but not ratified, the Cartagena Protocol. It has not signed (or ratified) the Nagoya Protocol, which requires a country to ratify the original Convention before it may become a signatory on the Nagoya Protocol.

Historically, the United States has voluntarily supported the Convention's programs financially and has implemented many of the recommendations of the Convention (though not the requirement to develop a national biodiversity strategy) under domestic statutes like the Endangered Species Act. Without treaty obligations, however, the United States' voluntary participation in the Convention can change with presidential administration.

Though the United States does not have a comprehensive national policy on biodiversity, there are a number of ways in which biodiversity is indirectly addressed and promoted by U.S. environmental law. Three such mechanisms are particularly worth noting: (1) statutes addressing particular aspects of biodiversity, including the protection of specific forms of wildlife and specific types of ecosystems, which can affect overall biodiversity; (2) specific policies adopted by individual federal agencies, which sometimes address biodiversity more directly (though these policies are subject to change with presidential administration); and (3) environmental assessments under NEPA, which often generate information regarding the impact of federal action on biodiversity. NEPA requires the environmental impacts of major government actions to be disclosed in environmental impact assessments.[6] These assessments often detail the impact of actions on the variety of life in an affected habitat or ecosystem, and sometimes trigger other legal requirements related to particular wildlife or ecosystem types.

Finally, a number of federal agencies have obligations to manage ecosystems in ways that affect biodiversity, and several of these have adopted biodiversity policies that direct their actions in the absence of more specific statutory directions or counter-orders from a President. The Agency for International Development, in particular, funds a number of projects in other countries to promote biodiversity.

Any strategy for ecosystem management necessarily impacts biodiversity—either by increasing or decreasing the health and viability of particular life-forms, as with wildlife law; or by increasing or decreasing the health and resilience of particular ecosystems, as with the protection of types of ecosystems (like wetlands) or specific ecosystems (such as the environs of Yosemite National Park). As a result, the general U.S. approach to ecosystem management—which focuses on protecting and preserving specific types of wildlife and ecosystems, and on preserving particular tracts of land for particular purposes—importantly impacts biodiversity.

TAKEAWAYS

✓ Regulation of biodiversity is challenging both scientifically and politically. From a scientific perspective, it is challenging to identify and understand the long-term and systemic impacts of changing or eliminating specific forms of life. From a political perspective, it can be difficult to know how much to prioritize biodiversity over competing values, like promoting development or supporting agriculture.

✓ The United States does not have a comprehensive national policy on biodiversity. It is also not a signatory to the Convention on Biological Diversity.

✓ The National Environmental Policy Act plays an important role in requiring agencies to develop information about the likely biodiversity impacts of government actions.

✓ Other biodiversity goals are served through specific protections of particular ecosystems, such as wetlands or public lands, or species, as through the Endangered Species Act.

DISCUSSION QUESTIONS

1. What is the value of biodiversity? Should, and could, biodiversity be monetized?
2. Can there ever be sufficient biodiversity? How might such a standard be set?
3. Who benefits from biodiversity?

WILDLIFE

DEFINITION

Wildlife are undomesticated animals that live in their natural habitats.

DISTINCTIVE CHALLENGES OF WILDLIFE REGULATION

In the United States, one of the most salient uses of federal wildlife law is the protection of endangered species: forms of life whose continued existence is imperiled. Other federal and state policies seek to protect species that have cultural or social value, or permit the purposeful hunting or killing of other forms of wildlife. Wildlife law can also indirectly protect species through the regulation of trade in these animals and their products.

As with other forms of ecosystem management, a fundamental challenge of wildlife law is the informational burden of determining how human behaviors are likely to affect the variety of forms of wildlife that the law might target. The burdens of identifying and understanding particular forms of life can be particularly great when those organisms are rare or endangered, since by definition such organisms are fewer in number and thus often difficult to detect and study.

Another critical policy determination in wildlife law is the decision of which types of life to protect, and how much. The decision of which forms of life are valuable, either to humans or intrinsically, is morally and ethically complex, and is generally informed by social and cultural values. As a result, different jurisdictions often come to very different outcomes in determining which forms of life deserve the most protection, and the level of protection those forms of life deserve. For example, in most jurisdictions, many more legal protections exist for animals than for plants, and management schemes to protect animals must account for the fact that they are mobile, frequently crossing property and even state lines. This complicates questions of property rights, jurisdiction, and interstate cooperation. Such concerns are heightened for particularly mobile life-forms, such as migratory birds.

Wildlife law can also pertain to the indirect protection of species through the regulation on trade in these animals and their products. This is most often done for species whose endangerment and hunting have high social salience; for example, the United States has a special law addressing eagles, which are widely viewed as a national symbol. However, the hunting of these animals, and the use of their products, also tends to have high cultural value, particularly for indigenous peoples. Moreover, these groups are often not the cause of underlying endangerment, which heightens the direct tension between contemporary preservation and indigenous traditions.

KEY U.S. LEGAL APPROACHES TO WILDLIFE MANAGEMENT

In modern U.S. law, federal wildlife protections are dominated by the Endangered Species Act (ESA), a powerful statute passed in 1973 that protects endangered and threatened animal and plant species from public and private threats. Other statutes—including the Wild Bird Conservation Act, the Marine Mammal Protection Act, and the Bald and Golden Eagle Protection Act—add additional protections for specific classes, orders, or species of wildlife, and there are also special statutory prohibitions of illegal trade in animals and plants. Agencies play a key role in enforcing each of these statutes.

The United States is also a party to several international agreements that can create separate obligations to protect wildlife, including the Migratory Bird Treaty between the United States and Canada and the multilateral Convention on International Trade in Endangered Species of Wild Fauna and Flora (CITES). It is rare for these agreements to form an independent basis for legal action in the United States, however, as most of their provisions must be translated into domestic statutes to take effect.

The U.S. Fish and Wildlife Service is the agency responsible for enforcing federal fish and wildlife laws, including by helping to administer the ESA, and by managing and restoring nationally significant fisheries and important ecosystems like wetlands. State laws also play a role in wildlife law and are particularly important in fish and game regulation. State laws typically limit what fish and game may be captured, who is permitted to capture them, and where and when capture may take place. State wildlife agencies generally issue licenses pursuant to these laws. Generally, even landowners who want to hunt or fish on their own land must secure licenses. Finally, hunting, fishing, and gathering activities on Indian reservations are largely—although not entirely[7]—managed by tribal governments, and some hunting and fishing rights were guaranteed by specific treaties between the United States and specific tribes.

Endangered Species Act

The ESA creates a series of powerful legal protections for animal and plant species that are categorized as endangered or threatened, and for protecting habitat that is critical to those species' survival. It is often viewed as one of the most powerful U.S. environmental laws.

PUBLIC OBLIGATIONS UNDER THE ESA

The statute authorizes the Secretary of Commerce (for marine species) or the Secretary of Interior (for other species) to declare species "endangered" or "threatened" and to identify "critical habitat" (table 8).

Importantly, in determining which species to list, the Secretary of Commerce or the Interior is not permitted to consider the potential economic implications of listing, though she is allowed to take economics and other practical concerns into account in designating the critical habitat. Currently listed species include over twenty-two hundred species of animals, insects, and plants.[8]

Once a species is listed, federal agencies may not take any action that is "likely to jeopardize the continued existence" of that species or "result in the destruction or adverse modification of [critical] habitat for those species."[9] When an agency proposes acting in a way that may affect listed species, the agency is required to consult with either the

TABLE 8

Key Definitions in the Endangered Species Act

Legal Terms	Definitions
Endangered	"In danger of extinction throughout all or a significant portion of its range"
Threatened	"Likely to become an endangered species within the foreseeable future throughout all or a significant portion of its range"
Critical habitat	"Geographic areas that contain features essential to the conservation of an endangered or threatened species and that may require special management and protection"

Fisheries Service (for marine species) or the Fish and Wildlife Service (for non-marine species) to determine whether the action is likely to jeopardize the species' existence or critical habitat.

The requirements of the ESA have been interpreted strictly, and apply even where there are significant economic consequences. Most famously, in the well-known environmental case *Tennessee Valley Authority v. Hill*, the U.S. Supreme Court enjoined the operation of a virtually completed federal dam—which had been authorized prior to the ESA's passage, and on which over $100 million had already been spent—because the Secretary of the Interior had determined that finalizing the dam would eradicate the endangered snail darter, a small and economically trivial fish that had only been discovered in the early 1970s.[10]

In response to *Tennessee Valley Authority v. Hill*, Congress passed a highly burdensome exemption process to the provisions of the ESA, which allows a committee of agency heads and representatives from affected states—commonly called the "God Squad" because of its authority to determine whether a species survives—to exempt a government action from the ESA under very unusual circumstances. In practice, these circumstances—which include that there is no reasonable and prudent alternative to the action; that benefits "clearly outweigh" costs; and that the action is of regional or national significance[11]—are so rare that the exemption has been invoked successfully only two times. This means that the ESA almost always effectively prohibits agencies from taking actions found to imperil listed species, even if the species is viewed as relatively unimportant, and even if the proposed action is relatively large and economically important.

Although the ESA is focused on particular species rather than ecosystems, its protection of critical habitat often confers significant protection on entire ecosystems in which imperiled species live. In addition to the Act's prohibition on government action that damages critical habitat, the ESA also forms the basis for management of the National Wildlife Refuge System, a federal network of lands and waters directed toward conserving, managing, and restoring species categorized as endangered under ESA. Administered by the Fish and Wildlife Service, the refuge system incorporates ninety-six million acres (388,000 km²) of federal land.

PRIVATE OBLIGATIONS UNDER THE ESA

The ESA also prohibits private actions that "take" endangered—though not threatened—species without a permit. The definition of *take* in ESA has been controversial; it clearly includes intentional activities, such as killing or shooting endangered animals, but it has also been interpreted by the Department of the Interior to include unintentional harming of endangered animals. Activities that impair essential behavioral patterns—such as breeding, feeding, or sheltering—are in this category of a taking.[12] Private actors who violate the ESA can be subject to both civil fines (up to $25,000 per violation) and criminal penalties (including up to a year in prison per violation) for knowingly violating the Act.

Other Wildlife Protection Statutes and Treaties

The United States also has a number of other wildlife protection statutes and treaties that are designed to offer special protection to wildlife that are deemed especially valuable (table 9). These statutes operate in addition to the ESA—an endangered sea mammal, for example, would be subject to protection under both the Marine Mammal Protection Act and the ESA.

TABLE 9

Important Federal Statutes and Treaties Affecting Wildlife

Law	Year Enacted	Target
Lacey Act	1900	Prohibits import, export, sale and acquisition of fish, wildlife, or plants (or their parts) that are illegally taken, possessed, transported, or sold
Migratory Bird Treaty Act	1918	Protects migratory birds between the United States and Canada by making it illegal to hunt, capture, or sell migratory birds or bird parts (such as feathers)
Bald and Golden Eagle Protection Act	1940	Protects the bald eagle (the U.S. national bird) and the golden eagle
Fish and Wildlife Act	1956	Creates a national policy for managing fish, shellfish, and wildlife as resources
Marine Mammal Protection Act	1972	Protects marine mammals (including whales, dolphins, seals, manatees, sea otters, and polar bears)
Convention on International Trade in Endangered Species of Wild Fauna and Flora	1972	Prohibits international trade that threatens endangered species
Endangered Species Act	1973	Protects endangered and threatened species of animals and plants from public and private actions
Wild Bird Conservation Act	1992	Protects exotic (non-indigenous) birds, by limiting imports of exotic bird species (particularly those common to the exotic bird trade)

TAKEAWAYS

✓ Wildlife law requires policymakers to prioritize which types of life to protect, and how much.

✓ U.S. wildlife protections are dominated by the Endangered Species Act, a powerful law that protects animals and plant species whose populations have been designated endangered or threatened.

✓ A number of other treaties and statutes protect particular species, including wild birds, marine mammals, and culturally important species like the Bald Eagle.

✓ The Fish and Wildlife Service is an important federal authority for implementing federal wildlife laws. States and Indian tribes also play an important role in regulating hunting and fishing.

DISCUSSION QUESTIONS

1. Is it more important to protect rare species, whose continued existence is endangered, or common species? Which is more likely to have significant ecosystem impacts: protecting rare or common species? Which type of species is more likely to be culturally important?

2. How stringently should protected species be protected? Is it wise to protect those species and their habitats regardless of the cost of the protection, as the Endangered Species Act generally does? If not, how much cost is too much?

3. How important is it to respect and maintain cultural practices surrounding wildlife, like hunting?

MANAGEMENT OF SPECIAL ECOSYSTEMS: WETLANDS

The United States is home to several special ecosystems that are rare (within the United States or globally) and/or that exhibit unique features that allow them to sustain life-forms that cannot survive elsewhere. The management of each of these systems poses particular challenges. To illustrate these challenges, this section sets out the U.S. management of wetlands, which receive special legal treatment in the United States.

DEFINITION

Wetlands are transitional ecosystems that form a link between land and water. Some types of wetlands, such as swamps, are wet throughout the year; other types of wetlands, such as some marshes, are only seasonally inundated.

DISTINCTIVE CHALLENGES OF WETLANDS MANAGEMENT

The management of wetlands poses several distinctive challenges.

First are the definitional difficulties. Legal regimes designed to deal with land or with water may struggle to deal with the combination of the two. Because wetlands are by definition transitions between land and water, it can be challenging to identify which legal protections apply to them. For example, most wetland protections in the United States originate in the Clean Water Act, which only applies to "waters of the United States" (see spotlight 16). This means that wetlands that do not constitute "waters of the United States" do not have the benefit of most federal legal protections.

Second, there are many types of wetlands, which provide a variety of different ecosystem services, have varying levels of complexity, have specific relationships with neighboring ecosystems, are more or

---

SPOTLIGHT 16. "WATERS OF THE UNITED STATES"

Recent years have seen continued controversy in the United States over the appropriate definition of "waters of the United States." The debate has particular relevance to wetlands, which exist at the intersection of water and land.

For many years, the Environmental Protection Agency and the Army Corps of Engineers defined the term broadly, but that interpretation was questioned in the Supreme Court case *Rapanos v. United States*, 547 U.S. 715 (2006). Post-*Rapanos*, the EPA has adopted different interpretations of the term under different Presidents, with President Obama's EPA favoring a much more inclusive definition (that protected far more wetlands) than President Trump's EPA, which has adopted a much narrower definition that does not include physically isolated or most seasonal wetlands. Under the Trump-era definition, for example, wet meadows and seasonal streams are not protected as waters of the United States.

---

less isolated from water sources, and may vary seasonally.[13] Marshes, for example, are periodically saturated with water and are populated by non-woody vegetation adapted to wet soil conditions. They may be tidal—occurring along coastlines and interacting with marine ecosystems—or nontidal. Nontidal marshes often occur in poorly drained depressions and floodplains along the edges of lakes and rivers, although they may also occur in areas isolated from larger bodies of water, as with "prairie potholes," which develop when water collects in pockmarks left on the landscape by glaciers; or "wet meadows," which are fed primarily by precipitation and so may be dry in the summer. Swamps are another type of wetland, fed primarily by surface water inputs, and typically dominated by trees and shrubs. Like marshes, they may be fed either by freshwater or by saltwater. Bogs—freshwater wetlands whose only water source is rainwater—are characterized by spongy peat deposits and provide habitats for many rare and endangered plants. One type of bog, called a pocosin, is found only on the Southeastern Coastal Plain of the United States.

Third, while wetlands inarguably provide a range of valuable eco-system services—including water filtration, nutrient cycling, disaster risk reduction, aesthetic and recreational values, and biodiversity—the relative valuation of these services in comparison to other socially desirable outcomes remains controversial. This issue has proven to be particularly challenging when wetlands conflict with agricultural uses, and it also presents a series of difficult questions when wetlands management involves the construction of new or replacement wetlands, which may provide several services well (e.g., water filtration and nutrient cycling) while struggling to provide others (e.g., biodiversity).

KEY U.S. LEGAL APPROACHES TO WETLANDS MANAGEMENT

For most of its history, the United States actively sought to eliminate its wetlands, which were often viewed as unhealthy and undesirable. Americans were successful in this endeavor, managing to fill or otherwise destroy over half of the nation's wetlands. Agricultural policies actively encouraged the conversion of wetlands into agricultural uses, and the draining of swamps and filling of marshes were widely viewed as improvements. It was not until the 1970s—with improved information about the substantial ecosystem services that wetlands provide—that U.S. policy changed to treat wetlands with special solicitude. Modern wetlands policy is further articulated in Executive Order 11,990, which directs the government to take action "to minimize the destruction, loss or degradation of wetlands, and to preserve and enhance the natural and beneficial values of wetlands."

The primary statutory source of U.S. law on wetlands is the Clean Water Act, first passed in 1972. CWA applies to "navigable waters," defined as "waters of the United States." The Act thus applies to wetlands only insofar as they meet that definition. Wetlands that qualify as "waters of the United States" are protected under CWA Section 404, which creates a permit regime that bans unpermitted discharges of "dredged or fill materials" into the waters of the United States (including protected wetlands).

The EPA has promulgated guidelines that the Army Corps of Engineers must follow in granting or denying Section 404 permits. Under these regulations, permits to fill wetlands are granted only where there is no practicable alternative that would have less adverse impact on the aquatic ecosystem.[14] Where adverse impacts will occur, the section requires "compensatory mitigation," which allows permittees to degrade one wetland in exchange for improving (or even creating) a different wetland. This can include restoring a previously existing wetland, enhancing an existing site, establishing a new aquatic site, or preserving an existing aquatic site. Permit-driven obligations can be satisfied through direct action by the permittee; through so-called "mitigation banks," which allow for restoration, creation, or enhancement of wetlands for the purpose of compensating for unavoidable impacts to wetlands elsewhere; and/or through in-lieu fee mitigation, whereby fees are collected for the purpose of improving or creating wetlands. The overall goal of these policies is to prevent any net loss of wetlands—though, again, the wetlands protected are only those that can fit into the definition of wetlands as "waters of the United States."

TAKEAWAYS

✓ Wetlands, transitional ecosystems between land and water, provide a number of ecosystem services and may qualify for special protection under U.S. law.

✓ Wetlands that qualify as "waters of the United States" are protected under Section 404 of the Clean Water Act, which requires a permit before wetlands may be dredged or filled.

DISCUSSION QUESTIONS

1. Which types of ecosystems deserve special protections? Why protect wetlands in particular? Do you personally value wetlands (such as swamps and bogs)? Should individuals' valuations of an ecosystem matter to how those ecosystems are protected?

2. Does it make sense to protect U.S. wetlands as "waters of the United States"?

LAND MANAGEMENT AND PUBLIC LANDS
DEFINITION

Public lands are specific portions of land (or water) set aside by public entities for a variety of public purposes. Public lands may include areas designated as parks, forests, or refuges, and there are generally limitations on their use, meant to protect the land (or water) and ensure that it can be used sustainably for its designated purpose. In the United States, substantial acreage is also administered in trust by the federal government for Indians and Indian tribes.

DISTINCTIVE CHALLENGES OF PUBLIC LAND MANAGEMENT

All human, animal, and plant life exists within multiple interconnected ecosystems, which provide a variety of ecosystem services that are valuable to people. To ensure that ecosystems continue to operate in ways people find valuable, policymakers can choose to regulate human behaviors that affect those ecosystems (for example, by regulating polluting behavior) and/or take over managing the physical spaces in which ecosystems are located.

Public land may be set aside for a wide variety of uses. Choosing which land to set aside, and for which use, can be challenging and even politically controversial. The selection of goals is likely to fundamentally affect the way that the ecosystem(s) on the land are managed—for example, public land set aside to generate productive forests may be managed to produce timber, rather than to promote biodiversity; whereas land set aside to conserve and protect endangered species would presumably be managed with no consideration of potential timber revenues. Another complication of public lands management is the designation of who will manage the land, and of the specificity of direction and strength of oversight.

Even after land has been designated for a particular use, and a public entity has been tasked with administering the land for that use, it can be challenging to determine the best management practices for achieving the relevant goals. This is particularly true where public land managers must manage the land to promote two or more purposes. The U.S. National Park Service, for example, is directed to accomplish two goals when administering the National Park System: "to conserve the scenery and the natural and historical objects and the wild life therein" and "to provide for the enjoyment of the same in such manner and by such means as will leave them unimpaired for the enjoyment of future generations." This dual mandate reflects a legislative compromise reached when the statute was passed, but it presents modern administrators with a continual puzzle of how to manage National Parks to allow them to be enjoyed and accessed by current populations, while simultaneously conserving them.

KEY U.S. LEGAL APPROACHES TO PUBLIC LANDS

The federal government administers a massive network of public lands that include a wide variety of ecosystems (see spotlight 17). The sheer expansiveness is striking: U.S. public lands cover more than a quarter of the total land mass of the United States (about the same land area as the entire country of India). The National Park System alone is the world's largest, both in number of sites (417) and in total land area. In addition, each state has a system of state parks, which also vary widely—from

(Paragraph continues on p. 178)

SPOTLIGHT 17. FEDERAL LAND MANAGEMENT SYSTEMS

Federal lands in the United States incorporate five different land management systems, which are administered by four different agencies. For each of these systems, federal agencies are the primary decision makers in determining how land will be managed. The majority of these lands are located in the western United States; 223.8 million acres are located in the state of Alaska alone.

The National Forest System, administered by the U.S. Forest Service, extends over 193 million acres (781,000 km^2) and is intended to "sustain the health, diversity, and productivity of the Nation's forests and grasslands to meet the needs of present and future generations." As administered, this land is primarily used to generate forest products, for domestic grazing, and as fish and wildlife habitat.

The National System of Public Lands, administered by the Bureau of Land Management, incorporates 264 million surface acres (1 million km^2) and 560 million subsurface acres (primarily in the West). These lands are intended to "sustain the health, diversity, and productivity of the public lands for the use and enjoyment of present and future generations." As administered, these lands are primarily used for mining, domestic grazing, timber, energy extraction, and fish and wildlife habitat.

The National Park System, administered by the National Park Service, includes 419 sites, sixty-two of which are designated as "National Parks," and extends over 84 million acres (340,000 km^2), about two-thirds of which is in Alaska. The purpose of the National Park System is to "conserve the scenery, the natural and historic objects, and the wildlife in the United States' National Parks, and to provide for the public's enjoyment of these features in a manner that will leave them unimpaired for the enjoyment of future generations," and the National Park Service administers the parks for conservation purposes. The Grand Canyon National Park, Yellowstone

National Park, and Yosemite National Park are probably the most famous, while the Great Smoky Mountains National Park, with over eleven million visitors annually, is the most visited.

The National Wildlife Refuge System, administered by the U.S. Fish and Wildlife Service, incorporates 567 national wildlife refuges and thirty-eight wetland management districts, spread over 96 million acres (388,000 km^2), 80 percent of which is in Alaska. This land is intended to "conserve, protect, and enhance fish, wildlife, plants, and their habitats for the continuing benefit of the American people." As administered, the National Wildlife Refuge System is used for wildlife and habitat conservation, as well as wildlife-related recreation, including hunting and fishing.

The National Wilderness Preservation System is administered by all four land management agencies and extends over 803 designated wilderness areas and 110 million acres (445 million km^2), about half of which is in Alaska. The purpose of the system is the "preservation and protection" of "wilderness" areas "in their natural condition," "for the use and enjoyment of the American people in such manner as will leave them unimpaired for future use and enjoyment as wilderness." Under the Wilderness Act of 1964, *wilderness* is defined as "an area where the earth and community of life are untrammeled by man, where man himself is a visitor who does not remain" and "an area of undeveloped Federal land retaining its primeval character and influence, without permanent improvements or human habitation, which is protected and managed so as to preserve its natural conditions." Accordingly, wilderness lands are administered to minimize human impact.

urban parks, to sprawling refuges on par with some National Parks, to game and recreation parks.

The Property Clause in the Constitution provides Congress the authority to acquire, dispose of, and manage federal property. Pursuant to a series of land management statutes issued by Congress, U.S. public lands are managed by four federal agencies—the Forest Service, the Bureau of Land Management, the Fish and Wildlife Service, and the National Park Service (figure 5). These agencies, while guided and constrained by their particular statutory mandates, also have substantial discretion in deciding how to manage the land under their control. Courts step in only rarely to second-guess agencies' determinations of best management practices.

The impact of agencies' management on the ecosystems of the land they administer varies significantly by purpose, and with individual agencies' interpretation of that purpose. The Bureau of Land Management, for example, is explicitly tasked with "management of public lands and their various resource values so that they are utilized in the combi-

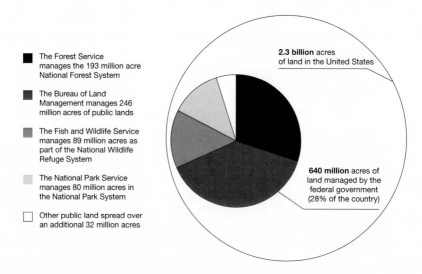

The Forest Service manages the 193 million acre National Forest System

The Bureau of Land Management manages 246 million acres of public lands

The Fish and Wildlife Service manages 89 million acres as part of the National Wildlife Refuge System

The National Park Service manages 80 million acres in the National Park System

Other public land spread over an additional 32 million acres

2.3 billion acres of land in the United States

640 million acres of land managed by the federal government (28% of the country)

Figure 5. Public Lands in the United States.

nation that will best meet the present and future needs of the American people," a direction that requires them to balance multiple potential human and ecological needs. The bureau has long interpreted this direction to permit wide-scale coal and mineral extraction, as well as grazing, on land it manages—uses that lead to significant ecosystem degradation. By contrast, the Fish and Wildlife Service, in administering the 560 sites of the National Wildlife Refuge System, prohibits the removal of any object (natural, historical, or archaeological) from the land.

In addition to public lands, the United States also administers a complex network of Indian lands, the combination of which is sometimes called "Indian country." The largest proportion of this land is 56.2 million acres held in trust by the federal government and administered as federal Indian reservations, which are areas of land reserved by or for a specific indigenous people to live on and use. Other lands, called "allotted lands," are remnants of reservations that were broken up by the U.S. government in the late nineteenth and early twentieth centuries. These lands—which amount to more than ten million acres—are held in trust for Indian allottees and their heirs. Some states also have state Indian reservations, which are lands held in trust by the state for an Indian tribe. Within Indian country, Indian tribes generally have rights of self-determination, though they are still subject to federal law. Within the constraints of federal law, however, various Indian tribes have substantial variation in the land management practices they implement in managing their lands.

TAKEAWAYS

✓ The U.S. government administers a massive network of lands. These include public lands, administered for the benefit of the public, and Indian lands, administered in trust for indigenous Indians and Indian tribes. In total, the federal government directly administers more than a quarter of the total land in the United States.

✓ Different public land systems are designed to serve different purposes, and thus are administered according to different goals. Types of public land include the National Forest System, the National System of Public Lands, the National Wildlife Refuge System, and the National Wilderness Preservation System.

DISCUSSION QUESTIONS

1. Does it make sense to have so many types of public land, administered for multiple different purposes and by multiple different agencies? What difficulties might you foresee arising from this complicated structure? Why might the structure nevertheless persist?

2. A large portion of U.S. land is directly managed by the federal government. What is the right amount of land to be managed by a national government? How can a government know when it has protected sufficient land and for the right purpose(s)?

AGRICULTURE
DEFINITION

Agricultural ecosystems are areas that are used for the growing of crops and the rearing of animals for food, fiber, and other products for human consumption. Agriculture purposefully prioritizes the interests of selected species—including agricultural crops, livestock, and tree crops—over other species, such as weeds and pests. Agricultural land use often infringes on, or entirely replaces, other land uses, such as habitats for wild animal and plant species. However, agricultural ecosystems can also provide habitats or sources of food for such animals. Agriculture operates as a powerful industry and serves a central role in maintaining food security.

DISTINCTIVE CHALLENGES OF REGULATING AGRICULTURE

Agriculture creates significant social value through the provision of food and other agricultural products. In addition, some people and groups attach value to the agricultural way of life, which is often seen as a counterbalance to an increasingly urbanized society, and which is sometimes held to have traditional cultural value. In the absence of agriculture, many rural areas would lose their main, or only, source of income.

Agriculture policy has important environmental impacts, as the quantity of land dedicated to cultivation of agricultural species potentially displaces other ecosystems and non-targeted species. Moreover, agricultural practices themselves can have important environmental impacts, especially through soil and water pollution. In turn, agriculture is fundamentally affected by many other ecosystem services, including water, soil erosion, soil quality, and climate.

A common tension in agricultural policy is between short-term productivity and long-term sustainability. One example of this is monocropping—the practice of growing a single crop year after year on the same land, in the absence of rotation through other crops or growing multiple crops on the same land. Monocropping allows farmers to specialize and to invest in crop-specific machinery, pest control, and growing methods, which makes it an economically highly efficient system. However, it damages soil ecology by depleting soil nutrients and provides a niche for parasitic species. As a result, monocropping leads to heightened dependence on pesticides and artificial fertilizers, both of which create negative environmental externalities. More generally, the use of pesticides (to boost crop production) contaminates soil, water, and other vegetation and can kill a wide variety of organisms, including non-targeted birds, fish, and plants.

Another challenge for agricultural policy is the increasing variability of production. Climate change has shifted precipitation and temperature patterns over much of the globe and is a key cause of variability in production. Importantly, while agricultural productivity can vary significantly from year to year as a result of weather and other conditions, the demand for food remains relatively stable. As a result, many countries have chosen to heavily subsidize food production, in hope that doing so creates a kind of margin of safety through overproduction to ensure that there is always sufficient food. In many cases, however, these subsidies introduce market distortions that lead to overcultivation of one or a few crops.

Finally, agricultural policy faces the puzzlesome question of which species to cultivate. This includes selection of specific species (such as corn) as well as trade-offs between animal and plant cultivation. In addition, agricultural policymakers face the question of what to do with GMOs—organisms that have been genetically modified to have some agriculturally desirable trait. Knowledge on the impact of these organisms on agricultural (and surrounding) ecosystems, and on humans through consumption, is still developing. As a result, different governments have adopted different regimes to deal with GMOs. Some, like the United States, permit a broad use of GMOs; while others, like the European Union, have banned their use almost entirely.

KEY U.S. LEGAL APPROACHES TO REGULATING AGRICULTURE

There are over two million farms in the United States, covering an area of 922 million acres (with an average size of 418 acres per farm). Corn and soybeans are the most common crops, making up about half of the planted farmland in the United States; most are grown using monocropping techniques. From an environmental perspective, the agriculture of the United States is often particularly noted internationally for its emphasis on monocropping and its substantial use of genetically engineered crops.

U.S. agriculture is a powerful industry. Agriculture, food, and related industries account for about 5.5 percent of the U.S. gross domestic product, or about a trillion dollars a year. The industry indirectly employs twenty-one million people, or 11 percent of total U.S. employment. Direct on-farm employment accounts for about 2.6 million of these jobs, or 1.3 percent of total U.S. employment.

The most important agricultural authority in the United States is the U.S. Department of Agriculture (USDA), which is charged with administering a series of agricultural laws and regulations,[15] which empower it to manage food policy and agricultural policy at a national level. Among other functions, the USDA administers a massive number of farm subsidies. These were originally intended to provide economic stability to farmers during the Great Depression of the 1930s, when policymakers were concerned about securing a steady domestic food supply despite dropping food prices. They have continued since then, however; nowadays, the USDA administers payments of about $25 billion annually to farmers and owners of farmland. The agency also administers a system of subsidized crop insurance, meant to protect farmers from insolvency during periods of drought or other disaster.

Agricultural activities can trigger obligations under a series of federal pollution control regimes, depending upon whether the activity involves management of toxic substances (such as pesticides) or whether it can be expected to cause pollution of air, water, or soil.[16]

The U.S. agricultural industry relies heavily on pesticides, fungicides, and other toxic substances to control pests. These are regulated largely through the Federal Insecticide, Fungicide, and Rodenticide Act,[17] which also regulates biopesticides, including genetically modified Bt toxins. If a crop is genetically engineered to carry Bt toxin, the EPA requires the developer to verify that the toxin is safe for the environment.

Agriculture in the United States, as elsewhere, is both a significant consumer of water and a significant contributor to water pollution. Importantly, the impacts of agricultural land use on water quality are largely excepted from the CWA, which is focused on regulation of "point source," channeled sources of water pollution, rather than the types of diffuse "nonpoint sources" typically created by agricultural runoff.[18] Nonpoint source water pollution, including agricultural runoff from fields and crop and forest lands, is instead regulated by the states. The EPA encourages—but does not require—states to establish "best management practices" for controlling nonpoint source water pollution. Perhaps unsurprisingly, states vary in how successful they are in establishing and enforcing such practices, and this structure struggles in addressing water bodies that border on multiple states. Many U.S. water systems have become substantially degraded by agricultural runoff as a result. One example is the Mississippi River, which runs from northern Minnesota, through the agricultural heartland of the United States, into the Gulf of Mexico. While the water quality of the upper Mississippi is pristine, as the river flows south, it receives such quantities of pesticide and fertilizer runoff from agriculture that by the time it reaches the ocean, the river is largely incapable of supporting life. Where the river feeds into the Gulf, it creates a "dead zone" of seven thousand square miles, one of the largest such zones in the world. Although most agricultural runoff is treated as nonpoint source water pollution, there is an important exception for "concentrated animal feeding operations" (CAFOs), sometimes called factory farms. Water quality impacts of CAFOs are regulated under the CWA, and operators of CAFOs are required to acquire permits under the National Pollutant Discharge Elimination System.

Policies addressing agricultural air pollution, such as can result from prescribed fires or from ammonia emissions from fertilizer and livestock waste, are slowly evolving. The USDA was required to establish a task force in 1996 to address agricultural air quality issues.[19] Since then, it has established some improvements in the reporting of agricultural air pollution data for conventional pollutants, which states then use in implementing the requirements of the Clean Air Act through their State Implementation Plans. Agricultural emissions of greenhouse gases amount to about 8 percent of U.S. greenhouse gas emissions, and U.S. agriculture faces significant challenges from changing climate conditions. As of this writing, however, there is no federal statutory scheme addressing agricultural climate emissions.[20] In the absence of federal legislation, agricultural climate policy is largely managed by regulatory agencies under the direction of the President, including the USDA, which administers several programs for agricultural climate change adaptation and, to a lesser extent, mitigation.[21] The United States is generally viewed as friendly to the use and cultivation of GMOs, and specifically to genetically modified crops. The first commercially grown genetically engineered food—the Flavr Savr tomato—was developed by the California company Calgene, and was approved by the U.S. Food and Drug Administration in 1994; the tomato went into production and was commercially available the same year. The United States has no general ban on the use of genetically modified organisms, and the Food and Drug Administration considers most GMO crops "substantially equivalent" to non-modified crops. A large proportion of the most commonly grown crops in the United States are now genetically engineered, including 90 percent of corn, 92 percent of cotton, and 94 percent of soybeans.[22]

TAKEAWAYS

✓ Agriculture is a substantial industry in the United States.

✓ Pollution from agriculture can trigger obligations under a number of federal pollution control regimes. In some cases, and particularly in the Clean Water Act, these statutes address agricultural pollution separately from other kinds of pollution. Notably, agricultural runoff is treated as nonpoint source water pollution, and thus is primarily managed by states rather than by the federal government.

✓ The U.S. Department of Agriculture is a key actor in regulating agriculture policy. Among other functions, it administers substantial agricultural subsidies.

✓ Insecticides and pesticides are regulated by the Federal
Insecticide, Fungicide, and Rodenticide Act.

✓ In the United States, genetically modified crops are
generally treated as substantially equivalent to non-modified
crops.

DISCUSSION QUESTIONS

1. Who should decide which species to cultivate—individual
landowners, states, or the federal government? How should the
government decide when and how to provide agricultural
subsidies?

2. Why might the drafters of the Clean Water Act have chosen to
leave agricultural water pollution to states to regulate? Given
that decentralized control of agricultural water pollution has
allowed for the substantial contamination of important waterways, should the United States reconsider its approach to
agricultural runoff?

3. Should genetically modified foods be regulated by national or
local actors?

ECOSYSTEM MANAGEMENT: SUMMARY

Ecosystem management in the United States reflects a series of normative choices about which ecosystems, and which qualities of ecosystems, deserve protection. Although the United States does not have a comprehensive national policy on biodiversity, and is not a party to the Convention on Biological Diversity, it does have a series of protections in place for particular ecosystems, such as wetlands, and strong protections for endangered animal and plant species through the Endangered Species Act. In addition, through the federal public lands system, the U.S. government directly administers over a quarter of the land in the United States, via multiple agencies tasked with maximizing different ecosystem qualities. Generally speaking, U.S. agricultural law and policy are administered separately from other environmental schemes.

KEY TERMS

BIODIVERSITY The variety of life in a habitat or ecosystem.

COMPENSATORY MITIGATION Allowing for the degradation of one habitat, such as a wetland, in exchange for improving (or even creating) a different habitat.

CONSERVATION The protection of a natural environment or species.

ECOSYSTEMS Geographic areas where living entities (plants, animals, and other organisms) and nonliving entities (water, air, and soil) interact in mutually interdependent ways.

GENETIC MODIFICATION The manipulation of an organism's genes using biotechnology, typically to augment desirable traits or delete undesirable ones.

HABITAT The home of an animal, plant, or other organism.

INDIAN The term used in the U.S. Constitution to refer to North American indigenous peoples.

INDIAN COUNTRY All lands in Indian reservations or held in trust for individual Indians or Indian tribes.

INDIAN RESERVATION An area of land reserved for an Indian tribe to live on and use.

NONPOINT SOURCE WATER POLLUTION Water pollution that originates from multiple diffuse sources, as from agricultural runoff or drainage through urban streets.

POINT SOURCE WATER POLLUTION Water pollution that originates from a single identifiable source, such as a pipe or ditch.

POTENTIALLY RESPONSIBLE PARTY (PRP) Under CERCLA, a person or company—including past and current owners—who may be responsible for cleanup costs for a contaminated site.

SUSTAINABILITY The use of natural resources in a way that is economically, socially, and environmentally viable in the long term.

WETLANDS Transitional ecosystems that form a link between land and water.

WILDERNESS An area of land that exhibits minimal human impact; in the United States, such lands are protected under the National Wilderness Preservation System.

WILDLIFE Undomesticated animals that live in their natural habitats.

DISCUSSION QUESTIONS

1. Do some ecosystems deserve more protection than others? Why or why not?

2. Who should decide which ecosystems to protect? Are ecosystems more a local, national, or international concern?

NOTES

1. See Robert Lackey, *Seven Pillars of Ecosystem Management,* 40 LANDSCAPE & URBAN PLANNING 21–30 (1998).

2. This term was first introduced in Study of Critical Environmental Problems (SCEP), MAN'S IMPACT ON THE GLOBAL ENVIRONMENT (MIT Press 1970).

3. See United Nations, ECOSYSTEMS AND HUMAN WELL-BEING: SYNTHESIS ("Millennium Ecosystem Assessment") (2005), www.millenniumassessment .org/documents/document.356.aspx.pdf.

4. For a description of arguments that ecosystems have intrinsic value separate from their value to humans, see Ronald Sandler, *Intrinsic Value, Ecology, and Conservation,* 3 NATURE EDUC. KNOWLEDGE, no. 10, 2012: 4.

5. Full text available at www.cbd.int/convention/text/default.shtml.

6. See spotlight 11 in chapter 4.

7. Notably, provisions of the Endangered Species Act have been read to apply to (some) Indian lands. For a discussion of the complex and evolving role of the ESA in Indian country, see Marren Sanders, *Implementing the Federal Endangered Species Act in Indian Country,* Joint Occasional Paper on Native Affairs No. 2007–01 (2007).

8. The Fish and Wildlife Service maintains an updated list of protected species at www.fws.gov/endangered/species/index.html.

9. ESA § 7 (2).

10. See *Tennessee Valley Authority v. Hill,* 437 U.S. 153 (1978).

11. See 16 U.S.C. § 1536(h)(1)(A).

12. See 50 CFR § 17.3 (1994). This regulation has been in place since 1975 and was famously upheld as an acceptable interpretation of the Endangered Species Act in the Supreme Court case of *Babbitt v. Sweet Home Chapter of Communities for a Greater Oregon,* 515 U.S. 687 (1995).

13. See Environmental Protection Agency, *Types of Wetlands,* EPA 843-F-01–002b (2001), https://nepis.epa.gov/Exe/ZyPDF.cgi?Dockey=200053PZ.PDF.

14. See 40 C.F.R. § 230.010(a)–(d). Permits are also prohibited if they would contribute to the violation of a state water quality standard; would cause or contribute to significant degradation of the waters of the United States, unless appropriate and practicable steps have been taken that will minimize potential adverse impacts of the discharge on the aquatic ecosystem; or are contrary to the public interest.

15. The USDA keeps a list of laws and regulations it administers at www .usda.gov/our-agency/about-usda/laws-and-regulations.

16. The EPA maintains a list of environmental laws and regulations that apply to various agricultural activities at www.epa.gov/agriculture/laws-and-regulations-apply-your-agricultural-operation-farm-activity.

17. See chapter 6 for more detail on FIFRA.

18. See chapter 6 for more detail on the CWA.

19. See USDA Agricultural Air Quality Task Force, at www.nrcs.usda.gov /wps/portal/nrcs/main/national/air/taskforce/.

20. See chapter 8 for further discussion of U.S. climate change law and policy.

21. For an overview of the USDA's approach to climate change and agriculture, see U.S. Department of Agriculture, "Climate Solutions," www.usda .gov/topics/climate-solutions.

22. The USDA maintains records on the adoption of genetically engineered crops. They report recent numbers at www.ers.usda.gov/data-products/adoption-of-genetically-engineered-crops-in-the-us/recent-trends-in-ge-adoption. aspx.

CHAPTER EIGHT

Climate Change

This chapter provides a primer on the U.S. legal approach to regulating climate change. It outlines regulatory challenges, presents some background about historical and current emissions, discusses the predicted impacts of climate change on the United States, and describes the fundamentals of the current U.S. approach to managing climate change—an approach that relies heavily on domestic law.

CLIMATE CHANGE AS AN ENVIRONMENTAL PROBLEM

Climate change is any significant change in weather—in temperature, precipitation, wind, or other effects—that lasts for a significant period. While some changes in climate are part of the natural environment, when changes in climate are sudden and extreme enough to outpace the speed of natural selection and other natural processes, they can lead to mass extinctions and even to complete ecosystem collapse. This can negatively affect—even devastate—species and ecosystems that cannot adapt, and can also cause great human suffering, particularly among the world's most vulnerable populations, who face special challenges in adapting to changing conditions.

Until the Industrial Revolution, periodic changes in climate were mostly caused by natural phenomena, such as solar flares or volcanic activity. Greenhouse gases (GHGs), including carbon dioxide (CO_2), were emitted through nonhuman processes (such as plant matter decay) and absorbed through other nonhuman processes (for instance, through absorption into the oceans). Plants, animals, and ecosystems adapted to gradual changes in climate and, over millennia, developed into the rich, biodiverse mosaic of life that now populates the planet.

Starting in the Industrial Revolution, however, humans began emitting increasing quantities of GHGs—significantly more than can be absorbed by natural processes. Most of these emissions come from burning fossil fuels like coal and oil. When more GHGs are emitted than are absorbed, the remainder ends up in the atmosphere. The current level of GHGs in the atmosphere is causing changes in weather patterns that are so severe and rapid that they will likely have devastating consequences for human, animal, and plant life.

Experts generally agree that reversing anthropogenic climate change is no longer possible. To mitigate some of the impacts, actions must be taken to reduce GHG emissions. At the same time, adaptation strategies are needed to deal with some of the unavoidable effects of climate change.

Since the global community became aware of climate change in the early 1970s, it has proven extremely difficult to translate the need for climate change mitigation and adaptation into meaningful regulatory action. There are several reasons for this (see spotlight 18).

First, climate change has a multitude of diffuse causes; every human action (including breathing!) results in the emission of some GHGs, and it would not be possible, or desirable, to regulate each of these activities. Moreover, those who benefit from GHG-emitting activities—such as through industrial activity—do not necessarily shoulder the costs of climate change. The effects of climate change are also diffuse through space and time: GHG emissions anywhere in the world add to the total stock of emissions that may result in negative consequences anywhere in

---

SPOTLIGHT 18. KEY CHALLENGES
IN CLIMATE CHANGE POLICY

Important challenges to the formation of effective climate change
policy include

- varied impacts across stakeholders, across borders, and
  through time;
- complex science from multiple disciplines with multiple
  sources of uncertainty; and
- coordinating multiple actors who have differing past and
  present causal responsibility, different expected impacts,
  and different interests.

---

the world, and the effect of current emissions may not be felt until fifty
to a hundred years from now. The fact that people can externalize the
costs of their current behavior—costs to be borne by future generations
and by others living in other parts of the world—makes it difficult to
incentivize them to change that behavior.

Second, although the science connecting human emissions of GHGs
to climate change is now uncontroversial within the scientific community,[1] it is challenging to tie individual actions that cause climate
change to specific impacts (see spotlight 19). The actual pattern of climate change—its severity, time, scale, and scope—is almost overwhelmingly complex. Although there is widespread scientific consensus that the global climate is changing as a result of human activities,
there remains significant uncertainty regarding both short- and long-term consequences of those changes, complicated by the interactive
qualities of many nonhuman processes and ecosystems. These uncertainties are further exacerbated by the question of how humans
will change their mitigation and adaptation behaviors in the coming
years.

SPOTLIGHT 19. CLIMATE SCIENCE

Predicting the timing and location of climate change effects is complex, and the science around climate change has been subject to much controversy. The main international body dealing with these questions is the Intergovernmental Panel on Climate Change (IPCC), an international panel of more than thirteen hundred scientists and experts. Its reports (freely available on www.ipcc.ch) are the result of rigorous scientific research. Because these reports form the basis for international negotiations on climate change, they are subject to approval and adoption by the countries that are party to the United Nations Framework Convention on Climate Change, including the United States. While this increases their legitimacy in the eyes of many, this process has also met with criticism suggesting that the published outcomes are subject to political processes.

In the United States, the U.S. Global Change Research Program develops and coordinates a national research program for understanding and predicting climate change impacts. Established by executive order in 1989, and mandated by Congress in the Global Change Research Act of 1990, the program builds on and coordinates with the scientific research of the IPCC, and coordinates and integrates additional research at thirteen federal agencies. The program issues periodic National Climate Assessments (all available at www.globalchange.gov) evaluating expected impacts of climate change within U.S. borders.

Third, the ultimate extent of climate change's impact on nonhuman entities and processes is expected to be devastating, which in turn will create high human costs. However, in calculating these nonhuman and human costs, the complexity and uncertainty surrounding climate change can make it difficult for regulators to determine the appropriate stringency of costly mitigation and adaptation efforts.

Combined, these three characteristics of the causes and effects of climate change amount to the most "wicked" regulatory problem facing governments today.[2] While every person contributes to climate change in many small ways, no single person, state, or country can meaningfully mitigate climate change alone. This creates two additional problems: a *collective action problem*, in which effective mitigation of climate change necessitates action by a multitude of individual countries; and a *free-rider problem*, in which each country prefers to have mitigation and adaptation paid for by other countries.

Moreover, past GHG emissions were largely driven by the industrial development of developed countries, whereas future GHG emissions are expected to be largely driven by the industrial development of developing countries. Perhaps understandably, developing countries—which are likely to be more severely affected by climate change—are unwilling to limit their chance for socioeconomic development by halting or significantly slowing industrialization. These complicated questions of how to balance the profits of past emissions (by some) with the costs of future climate change (for others), while considering the need for development of future generations, is often thought to make international collaboration on this topic almost impossible.

CLIMATE CHANGE IN THE UNITED STATES: CAUSES, IMPACTS, AND ATTITUDES

Causal Contributions

Historically speaking, the United States has emitted more atmospheric GHGs than any other nation (figure 6).[3] From the early nineteenth century, emissions grew particularly rapidly in the relatively industrialized Northeast, and grew still further with the advent of petroleum-powered automobiles. Today, the United States emits more CO_2 each year than every country in the word except China (figure 7). U.S. emissions peaked around 2005; by 2015, that level had been reduced by about 12 percent.[4]

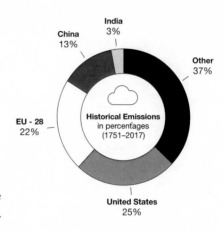

Figure 6. Historical Greenhouse
Gas Emissions.

Per capita U.S. emissions (at 16.5 metric tons per person per year) remain the highest of any developed economy (figure 8). Countries with higher per capita emissions—such as Qatar (35.73), Bahrain (21.8), United Arab Emirates (19.3), and Saudi Arabia (16.54)—are mostly those whose economies depend heavily on fossil fuel extraction and refinement.[5]

Within the United States, emissions vary enormously by state, ranging from 7.1 metric tons (Vermont) to 873.8 metric tons (Texas). In fact, ten of the fifty states are responsible for nearly half of national emissions.[6] Per capita emissions also vary significantly: the lowest state per capita rates vie with the lowest in the world; in Vermont, for example, per capita emissions amount to 0.11 metric tons. By contrast, states with substantial natural gas, coal, and petroleum activity—such as Wyoming, North Dakota, and West Virginia—have particularly high per capita emissions rates (170.6, 120.5, and 52.5 metric tons, respectively). Throughout the United States, the energy sector is responsible for the majority (84 percent) of emissions, with agriculture (8 percent), industrial processes (4 percent), and other sources (4 percent; primarily waste management) constituting the remainder.

Within the energy sector, electric power—which in the United States is largely provided by natural gas and coal combustion[7]—is the largest contributor, making up 29 percent of the nation's total emissions.

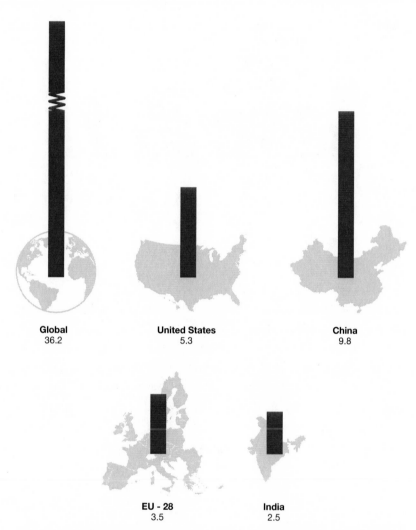

Figure 7. Annual Greenhouse Gas Emissions (Total Emissions in Billions of Metric Tons per Year, 2017).

Transportation (27 percent), industrial power use (15 percent), and residential energy use (5 percent) are also significant contributors.[8] Of these, transportation—which is expected to rely increasingly on electric vehicles—is expected to soon overtake electric power as the primary driver of energy-based emissions.

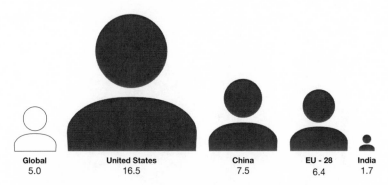

Global	United States	China	EU - 28	India
5.0	16.5	7.5	6.4	1.7

Figure 8. Per Capita Greenhouse Gas Emissions (Metric Tons per Person per Year, 2014).

Current and Expected Impacts

The United States, like the rest of the world, is already experiencing some impacts from climate change. These include shifting plant and animal ranges, lengthening growing seasons, loss of sea ice and glaciers, increasing frequency and magnitude of natural disasters, and accelerated sea-level rise. The Intergovernmental Panel on Climate Change (IPCC)—an international panel of more than thirteen hundred scientists and experts— provides forecasts of the impacts of climate change. As in the rest of the world, wealthier regions of the United States (such as the Northeast and Northwest) are likely to suffer relatively less from climate disruption, because they have a greater capacity to invest in adaptation. Poorer regions (such as the Southeast and Southwest) are likely to suffer relatively more, because of limited adaptive capacity. Within the United States, the U.S. Global Change Research Program's National Climate Assessments have predicted specific regional impacts (figure 9).[9]

Public Attitudes toward Climate Change

The American public has complicated attitudes about climate change, and individuals vary significantly in how they think about the issue.

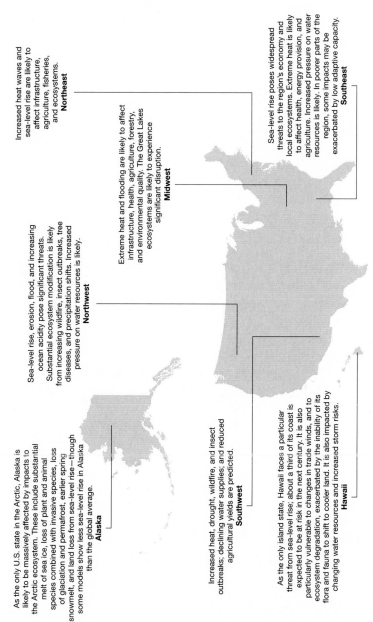

Alaska

As the only U.S. state in the Arctic, Alaska is likely to be massively affected by impacts to the Arctic ecosystem. These include substantial melt of sea ice, loss of plant and animal species combined with invasive species, loss of glaciation and permafrost, earlier spring snowmelt, and land loss from sea-level rise—though some models show less sea-level rise in Alaska than the global average.

Northwest

Sea-level rise, erosion, flood, and increasing ocean acidity pose significant threats. Substantial ecosystem modification is likely from increasing wildfire, insect outbreaks, tree diseases, and precipitation shifts. Increased pressure on water resources is likely.

Southwest

Increased heat, drought, wildfire, and insect outbreaks; declining water supplies; and reduced agricultural yields are predicted.

Hawaii

As the only island state, Hawaii faces a particular threat from sea-level rise; about a third of its coast is expected to be at risk in the next century. It is also particularly vulnerable to changes in trade winds, and to ecosystem degradation, exacerbated by the inability of its flora and fauna to shift to cooler land. It is also impacted by changing water resources and increased storm risks.

Midwest

Extreme heat and flooding are likely to affect infrastructure, health, agriculture, forestry, and environmental quality. The Great Lakes ecosystems are likely to experience significant disruption.

Northeast

Increased heat waves and sea-level rise are likely to affect infrastructure, agriculture, fisheries, and ecosystems.

Southeast

Sea-level rise poses widespread threats to the region's economy and local ecosystems. Extreme heat is likely to affect health, energy provision, and agriculture. Increased pressure on water resources is likely. In poorer parts of the region, some impacts may be exacerbated by low adaptive capacity.

Figure 9. Projected Impacts of Climate Change in the United States, by Region.

Recent studies suggest that most Americans recognize that global warming is happening; in one study, only 18 percent said that it is not, though almost a quarter remained unsure.[10] In the same study, a majority of Americans reported that they are "worried" about climate change, although other international surveys have suggested that climate change ranks comparatively low on Americans' general environmental concerns (e.g., fewer than 10 percent of Americans believe that climate change is the most important problem for the United States as a whole).[11] Americans who do not believe that climate change is happening are more than twice as likely to be politically conservative, and to align with the politically conservative Republican party, than the general American population.[12] Americans are more likely to perceive climate change as a personal threat when they believe that it is human-caused, when they experience local temperature changes, and when they support government efforts to preserve the environment.[13] As of this writing, it is unclear whether or how the coronavirus pandemic will affect Americans' perception and treatment of climate change risks.

INTERNATIONAL LAW AND CLIMATE CHANGE

Because the causes and effects of climate change are global, uncoordinated domestic approaches to mitigation are widely viewed as unlikely to be successful. For most countries in the world, climate change policy is therefore significantly affected by the terms of international climate change agreements, of which there are many.

By far the most important international climate law is the United Nations Framework Convention on Climate Change (UNFCCC), of which the United States is a member. Signed and ratified in 1992, the UNFCCC sets out the framework within which international climate negotiations take place. It has near-universal membership—197 countries as of December 2015—and the parties to the Convention meet annually to negotiate additional agreements, or protocols, that work toward the UNFCCC's aim of "stabilizing GHG concentrations in the atmosphere at a level that would prevent dangerous anthropogenic interference with the climate system."[14] The UNFCCC does not set out any binding limits on GHG emissions for the parties; rather, it obliges parties to create national inventories, which can help establish baselines for such binding limits. As in any area of international law, a significant challenge of using international law to address climate change is the question of enforcement. In the climate change context, this often manifests in disagreements between countries as to whether the targets set in climate agreements should be binding or voluntary. Thus far, the only climate agreement that has established binding obligations to reduce emissions is the 1997 Kyoto Protocol, which the U.S. signed but did not ratify; the Protocol established binding obligations for GHG reductions in developed countries for the period 2008–12. The 2015 Paris Agreement, by contrast, relies on procedural commitments to encourage countries to reduce emissions.

Negotiating international agreements to address climate change requires coordinating multiple actors that have differing past and present causal responsibility, different expected impacts, and different interests. Even starting on such negotiations can be challenging, which makes a framework for negotiations, such as the one provided by the UNFCCC, particularly valuable. Even with such a framework, questions about the timing and the relative responsibility of developing and developed nations remain perennially thorny. International climate agreements must also find some way to manage the scientific uncertainty involved in modeling climate impacts and predicting the effects of proposed behavioral changes.

The U.S. Approach to International Law on Climate Change

U.S. climate law—unlike that of most countries in the world—is mostly domestic. Although it remains a member of the UNFCCC, the United States has repeatedly refused to ratify international climate change agreements, such as the Kyoto Protocol and the Paris Agreement, that would commit it to reducing emissions (table 10).

TABLE 10

Important International Climate Change Agreements

Agreement	Year	Ratified by the United States?
United Nations Framework Convention on Climate Change	1992	Yes
Kyoto Protocol	1997	No
Paris Agreement	2015	No
Kigali Amendment to the Montreal Protocol	2016	Under consideration at time of press

Although the United States was active in the UNFCCC negotiation processes that led to the Kyoto Protocol—which was signed by 192 countries—it chose in the end not to ratify it. U.S. nonparticipation was widely viewed as a significant weakness in the agreement, as was the Protocol's structure, which applied emissions limitations only to developed (and not to developing) countries. Numerous efforts to conclude a new agreement to replace the Kyoto Protocol failed, until the Paris Agreement was adopted in 2015.

The Paris Agreement was important for several reasons. First, it built on the structure of the UNFCCC to clarify what "dangerous anthropogenic climate change" looks like, by stating a clear commitment to limit global temperature rises to 2°C.[15] Second, it puts in place procedural commitments for the parties to create "nationally determined contributions," to prepare national plans to achieve the contributions to mitigation, and to report on them regularly. Importantly, however, these are not substantive commitments to a centrally determined level of GHG emission reductions, as was the case with the Kyoto Protocol. Instead, they merely mandate that countries develop procedures to achieve the goals of the agreement.

Although President Barack Obama signed an executive order in 2016 adopting the Paris Agreement, it was never ratified by the U.S. Senate. As a result, Obama's successor, Donald Trump, had the authority to unilaterally cancel U.S. participation. He announced his intention to do so in 2017, and the United States formally withdrew on November 4, 2020. As a result, among the 197 countries in the world, only three—Syria, Nicaragua, and the United States—have chosen not to participate in the Paris Agreement.

President Trump's decision to withdraw from the Paris Agreement was domestically and internationally controversial and was met with substantial resistance by many U.S. states, localities, and private organizations. Many of these committed to voluntarily comply with the terms of the Paris Agreement, despite the lack of national involvement. As a result of some of these subnational commitments, and of market forces that have contributed to reductions in coal consumption, U.S. emission levels were about 12 percent less in 2019 than in 2005. (The effect of coronavirus on national emissions remains unclear as of this writing.) This remains significantly short, however, of a reduction of 26–28 percent by 2025, which would have been required by the Paris Agreement.

Although the United States has refused to ratify many key agreements negotiated under the UNFCCC, it has ratified and effectively enforced other agreements with significant climate change impacts, including most notably the Montreal Protocol on Substances that Deplete the Ozone Layer. The Montreal Protocol sought to protect the ozone layer by controlling substances known to cause ozone depletion, particularly chlorofluorocarbons (CFCs) and hydrochlorofluorocarbons (HCFCs). Importantly, the Kigali Amendment of 2016 addresses hydrofluorocarbons (HFCs), a substitute for CFCs and HCFCs that does not imperil the ozone layer but that has an extraordinarily high global-warming potential; this amendment is expected to prevent up to half a degree Celsius of warming by 2100. As of this writing, the United States is still considering whether to join the Kigali Amendment.

The history of the UNFCCC shows that international legal agreements, although they may be necessary to ensure effective solutions to climate change, bring their own challenges. First, the dispersed causes and impacts of climate change make it difficult to reach consensus within the international community. Questions about the relative responsibility of developed nations like the United States and developing countries remain controversial, as do questions about the appropriate timing and extent of commitments. Second, as in any area of international law, a significant challenge of using international law to address climate change is the question of enforcement. Even for "binding" obligations, of which there are few, it is hard to find effective means of enforcement, as nations remain sovereign in their decision to fulfill these obligations and/or to withdraw from international agreements. Finally, although nations retain the sovereignty to enter into binding international agreements, the possibility of substantial subnational implementation—of both mitigation and adaptation plans—adds significant complexity, and in some cases can create a patchwork of policies that are hard to predict and challenging to integrate.

KEY CHARACTERISTICS OF REGULATING CLIMATE CHANGE IN THE UNITED STATES

The United States is widely viewed as a reluctant participant in international attempts to recognize and manage climate change. The U.S. Congress has adopted no overarching national climate policy, nor has it issued any directed climate change legislation. As a result, modern U.S. climate change policy is governed by relatively obscure sources of domestic American law: presidential action, agency action implementing statutes that were never specifically designed to address climate change, and judicial opinions. Finally, the lack of centralized federal policy leaves substantial room for subnational law and policy on climate change.

DISCUSSION QUESTIONS

1. Does the United States have a special obligation to respond to climate change, given its historical contribution to causes of climate change? Should current Americans be forced to pay for emissions by their parents and grandparents? Similarly, should future Americans be forced to pay for their parents' and grandparents' failure to mitigate further climate change?

2. Do you expect the coronavirus pandemic to affect greenhouse gas emissions? Should it be expected to affect U.S. vulnerability to climate change impacts? What about global vulnerability?

LEGAL SNAPSHOTS: CLIMATE CHANGE AND THE UNITED STATES

The next section provides a series of "snapshots" explaining how the United States manages climate change through (1) mitigation, (2) adaptation and natural hazards policy, and (3) subnational approaches.

MITIGATION

DEFINITION

Climate change mitigation seeks to limit the magnitude and rate of long-term climate change. Reducing anthropogenic GHG emissions is the most important method of mitigation.

DISTINCTIVE CHALLENGES OF CLIMATE CHANGE MITIGATION

In some respects, the mitigation of climate change through the reduction of anthropogenic GHG emissions is a relatively simple task. For mitigation purposes, the location of the emission reductions is irrelevant (though it might be relevant for the reduction of related environmental impacts, such as air pollution and related health risks), which theoretically opens up the opportunity of reducing emissions wherever in the world it is easiest and cheapest. Such low-hanging fruit may be found specifically in developing economies that rely heavily on polluting industries that can be made cleaner relatively cheaply by installing newer technologies. Similarly, deforestation—the second-largest source of GHG emissions—is a practice that people might be convinced to forgo if alternative economic opportunities are provided.

Unsurprisingly, the fact that the climate effects of GHG-emitting activities do not occur in the same location as emissions also poses significant challenges. It allows people to externalize the effects of their actions, offloading them to others—if one country fails to mitigate, the global consequences will be borne largely by other countries. Similarly, if a country does successfully mitigate, it is likely to reap only a small portion of the total benefits of reduced emissions. The potential to externalize also applies over time, as there is generally a delay between GHG emissions and their impacts on the climate (see spotlight 20). This temporal element adds to the difficulty of determining how to "price" the mitigation of effects that will emerge in fifty, one hundred, or two hundred years, as compared to the cost of mitigation today.

Another problem is that reductions in GHG emissions in one place are easily offset by increases in another location. This is likely to be a central challenge to climate policy in the years to come, because many populous countries are experiencing economic growth that relies heavily on GHG-emitting activities. Even if the main emitters of the past—including the United States and the European Union—reduce their emissions, the per capita increase in emissions of countries such as China can easily offset those reductions. This again presents difficult questions of politics and fairness, as many developing countries claim a right to economic development such as developed countries have enjoyed in the past. One partial solution to this problem may include "technology transfer" of clean technologies from developed to developing economies, so that the latter can "skip" the most polluting stages of growth. The UNFCCC, to which the United States is a party, encourages such transfer, and the Paris Agreement relies substantially upon technology transfer as a strategy.

Apart from limiting GHG emissions by reducing the use of fossil fuels through cleaner technologies or by reducing deforestation, countries can also focus on reducing the need for fossil fuels through use of renewable energy or increased energy efficiency. These initiatives can be undertaken unilaterally and thus are less dependent on international agreements, though their internal desirability may be limited by potential losses of economic advantage vis-à-vis other countries.

A final category of mitigation possibilities is the "capture" or sequestration of GHG emissions rather than their reduction. Some methods of GHG capture and storage, such as afforestation, are relatively well

SPOTLIGHT 20. DISCOUNTING

Policymakers are routinely faced with questions about how many of today's resources to spend to prevent future harms from climate change. Although the costs of mitigation are mostly borne immediately, the benefits from mitigation may not accrue for decades or even centuries.

Discounting is a method for determining the present value of a benefit or harm that is expected to accrue some time in the future. Typically, the sooner someone receives a benefit, the more valuable it is to them. This is because they get the enjoyment of the benefit for longer, have greater opportunity to invest their resources, and can make those resources grow over time. Conversely, being assured that you will receive a benefit in the distant future holds less value in the present.

Generally, the rate at which money is predicted to gain value (particularly through investment) determines the economic "discount rate." For example, if economists think that money can be invested at a 7 percent rate of return each year, they will choose a 7 percent discount rate to translate future money into its present value.

Calculating the present value of climate change harms—or the benefits of preventing those harms—is complicated by the long time horizons of these harms and benefits, and by the uncertainties in predicting them. High discount rates make even extreme future impacts look small in today's dollars. Very high discount rates can make it seem nonsensical to adopt any kind of mitigation strategy at all.

Discounting money is not controversial, though some commentators object to discounting environmental impacts. The United States routinely monetizes both the economic and environmental impacts of climate change through the calculation of what it calls the Social Cost of Carbon—a quantified estimate of the social, economic, and environmental harm caused by each unit of carbon dioxide emissions. The United States also routinely discounts future impacts, including climate impacts, to present value.

studied; others, such as fertilizing oceans with iron to promote the growth of CO_2-consuming plankton and algae, remain experimental and are far less well understood. The main advantage of such techniques is that they require little or no change in emissions behavior, since they rely on taking emitted carbon out of the atmosphere and storing it elsewhere. At the moment, most capture technologies remain costly, but this may change in the future.

KEY U.S. APPROACHES TO CLIMATE CHANGE MITIGATION

Conventional wisdom is that global climate change is too large a problem for any single country to solve on its own. As a result, the majority of countries around the world build their national policies on the basis of international climate agreements. The United States has chosen not to do that, meaning that its mitigation efforts are almost entirely driven by domestic law and domestic actors.

Notably, the U.S. legislative branch has thus far played only a limited role in U.S. law and policy on climate change. In the absence of binding international agreements ratified by the U.S. Congress and of any overarching statutory regime addressing climate change, federal climate change policy is driven substantially by three key actors: the President, administrative agencies, and courts. Within these relatively obscure areas of federal law, the "Social Cost of Carbon"—or the amount of harm that each unit of greenhouse gas is expected to cause— plays a central part in setting U.S. mitigation policy (see spotlight 21). It is particularly important for providing a starting point for calculations of the appropriate stringency of mitigation strategies.

Domestic Legislation

The United States has no major federal legislation designed to address climate change. There are a number of statutes and statutory provisions

SPOTLIGHT 21. SOCIAL COST OF CARBON

The Social Cost of Carbon (SCC) is a quantified estimate of the social, economic, and environmental harm caused by each unit of carbon dioxide emissions. Some policymakers have called it "the most important number you've never heard of."

The SCC is now routinely used in regulatory cost-benefit analyses to determine how much mitigation efforts are cost-justified. Higher estimates of social cost justify more stringent laws, while lower estimates justify less stringency. Agency actions that failed to account for the impact of carbon emission reductions have been struck down as "arbitrary and capricious" by courts, so some estimate of the SCC is presumed to be required by courts.

In 2009, President Obama brought together a group of technical experts in an interagency working group (IWG) to identify a centralized, defensible estimate of the SCC to be used across federal agencies. Based on the global harm caused by each ton of carbon dioxide emission, the IWG developed a centralized estimate of about forty dollars per ton.

From 2009 to 2017, federal agencies used the IWG's estimate of the SCC to inform the stringency of regulations across a wide variety of topics, ranging from fuel efficiency in cars to energy conservation in refrigerators. In 2017, however, President Trump reversed Obama-era guidance to use the IWG's centralized global estimates of the SCC. Trump-era agencies have developed lower estimates, in large part by changing the scope to estimate only domestic impacts; these estimates have ranged from about two to eleven dollars per ton. As a general matter, larger estimates of the SCC are likely to justify greater regulatory stringency, whereas lower estimates are likely to justify laxer standards. As a result of using lower estimates of the SCC, Trump-era cost-benefit analyses justify significantly fewer emission reductions than Obama-era cost-benefit analyses.

with some climate change impacts, including the Global Change Research Act of 1990, which established the U.S. Global Change Research Program as a centralized point for integrating national research on climate change. Generally, however, in the absence of any comprehensive climate legislation, the statute with the greatest impact on federal climate mitigation policy is the Clean Air Act (CAA). The CAA was passed in 1970, before there was any significant science on anthropogenic climate change, and the EPA has faced difficulties in finding ways to apply the terms and structure of the CAA to GHGs. For example, the statute directs the Administrator of the EPA to regulate air pollutants that "cause, or contribute to, air pollution which may reasonably be anticipated to endanger public health or welfare." From 2003 until 2007, the EPA contended that GHGs were not air pollutants under the statute and, therefore, that it did not have the authority to regulate them. However, the Supreme Court rejected that argument in the landmark decision of *Massachusetts v. Environmental Protection Agency*, holding that GHGs "fit well within the Act's capacious definition of 'air pollutant,'" and demanding that the EPA determine whether or not GHGs may reasonably be anticipated to endanger public health or welfare—the portion of the statutory standard commonly called an "endangerment finding." The EPA issued an endangerment finding in 2009, finding that current and projected levels of six GHGs (CO_2, methane, nitrous oxide, hydrofluorocarbons, perfluorocarbons, and sulfur hexafluoride) endanger public health and welfare. The EPA also issued a "cause or contribute" finding that motor vehicles contribute to GHG emissions, and adopted limitations on new vehicle engines and vehicles. In addition, the EPA now maintains a Greenhouse Gas Reporting Program,[16] a database that provides comprehensive nationwide emissions data for large sources of GHGs. However, GHGs remain unregulated by the keystone of the CAA—the National Ambient Air Quality Standards—and further EPA attempts to regulate sources of CO_2 have met with inconstant presidential support, as discussed below.

Presidential Climate Law and Policy

In the absence of substantial international climate agreements ratified by Congress or of substantial domestic climate legislation, Presidents have significant power to shape U.S. climate policy. The two most recent Presidents—Obama and Trump—have taken substantially divergent approaches to climate change policy.

Obama, who was President from 2009 to 2017, took aggressive domestic action on climate change, implementing wide-ranging climate change policies through executive orders, a form of presidential action that does not require congressional approval. Perhaps the most important of these actions was the first Presidential Climate Action Plan, issued in 2013.[17] This plan recognized the existing and expected impacts of climate change on the United States and directed agencies to create both mitigation and adaptation plans. It also presented a more international view of the U.S. role in international climate policy than had previously characterized U.S. policy.[18] As already mentioned, in line with his emphasis on international cooperation, Obama also sought to use an executive order to implement the Paris Agreement. In one particularly influential move, he required agencies to address the global costs of climate change in their regulatory cost-benefit analyses, by requiring them to account for the Social Cost of Carbon. This led, in many cases, to the adoption of more stringent, climate-driven regulations. Under the direction of Obama, the EPA also adopted a broad reading of its authority under the CAA to regulate sources of GHG emissions, including the Clean Power Plan, a regulation intended to govern old power plants that had been exempted from regulatory requirements in the past, and issued a Climate Change Adaptation Plan attempting to identify strategies for the EPA to implement in promoting adaptation throughout the country.

Trump, who was elected President in 2016, has periodically evinced skepticism about climate science and has acted to unwind most of Obama's prior climate policies. He announced the intent to withdraw from the Paris Agreement, which had not been ratified by the U.S. Congress, in 2017; and, under his direction, the EPA has sought to formally unwind many of the regulations promulgated under the Presidential Climate Action Plan, including the Clean Power Plan. Trump also used executive orders to repudiate Obama's approach to estimating the Social Cost of Carbon. Under his direction, agencies have adopted much lower estimates of the likely harm of climate change, justifying these reductions in two ways: by limiting the scope of their estimates to impacts on the United States, rather than the world; and by adopting higher "discount rates" for future harms, an approach to valuation that makes future impacts look smaller in today's dollars. More informally, Trump has also backed away from the Obama-era Climate Change Adaptation Plan.

Unless the United States ratifies a climate agreement or the Congress adopts climate legislation, Presidents are likely to continue to have substantial power in shaping the climate policy of the United States. As a result, U.S. climate policy is particularly political and subject to change with presidential elections. That said, presidential power over climate policy is not unrestrained, even in the face of congressional silence. The President's authority is limited by courts, which act as arbiters of the constitutional separation of powers, help ensure that agencies directed by the President follow the statutory dictates of Congress, and continue to apply judicial common law.

Agency Action on Climate Change Law and Policy

Among all federal agencies, the EPA has the greatest set of statutory responsibilities regarding climate change. These stem from the CAA, which has been understood—since *Massachusetts v. EPA* and the EPA's endangerment finding—to require the EPA to regulate GHGs. The EPA has yet to issue a National Ambient Air Quality Standard for CO_2, though it has taken action to regulate mobile emissions from vehicles, the portion of the statute that was initially challenged in *Massachusetts v. EPA*. The EPA also administers several databases that provide information about emissions. Perhaps the most important of these is the nationwide Greenhouse Gas Reporting Program, which mandates reporting of emissions from large sources (which, in general, emit 25,000 metric tons or more of CO_2 equivalent per year in the United States). The program generally allows emitters to compute their own GHG emissions using any of several permissible methods; reports are then submitted to the EPA and compiled in a publicly available database.[19] The EPA also administers the Inventory of U.S. Greenhouse Gas Emissions and Sinks, which provides the official estimate of national GHG emissions.

Some other agencies also have climate-specific requirements, particularly regarding information collection and integration. The U.S. Global Change Research Program, for instance, coordinates climate research, while the National Oceanic and Atmospheric Administration (NOAA) has a series of obligations, including administering the national weather service, evaluating climate-related risks of drought and flood, and maintaining a database on climate and environmental information at the National Centers for Environmental Information.[20]

Finally, even federal agencies without specific statutory mandates often address climate change impacts through two general legal mechanisms. First, and possibly most importantly, agencies performing cost-benefit analyses routinely account for the expected climate impacts of their actions by using a quantified estimate of the Social Cost of Carbon.[21] Although the Social Cost of Carbon may seem technical, it importantly informs the stringency of many environmental regulations, where agencies must often show that the benefits of their proposed actions justify the costs.

Second, agencies considering actions that may substantially affect the environment are required to satisfy the terms of the National Environmental Policy Act (NEPA), which requires an assessment of environmental impacts prior to government action. For several years, the

---

SPOTLIGHT 22. INFLUENTIAL CLIMATE CASES

Massachusetts v. EPA, 549 U.S. 497 (2007)—A Supreme Court case
holding that if the EPA found that greenhouse gases endangered
public health and welfare, it was required to regulate greenhouse
gases as air pollutants under the Clean Air Act. This was the first
major federal requirement to address greenhouse gases.

*Center for Biological Diversity v. National Highway Transportation Safety
Administration*, 538 F.3d 1172 (9th Cir.) (2008)—A federal appellate
court case holding that a transportation agency that monetized
the impacts of greenhouse gas emissions (i.e., the social cost of
carbon) at zero dollars was acting arbitrarily and capriciously.
This case, and others with similar holdings, suggest that courts
will not allow agencies to unreasonably ignore climate impacts in
their cost-benefit analyses.

American Electric Power Co. v. Connecticut, 564 U.S. 410 (2011)—
A Supreme Court case holding that the Clean Air Act, by requiring
federal regulation of greenhouse gases, displaces federal
common law tort suits related to greenhouse gas emissions. By
interpreting the CAA to foreclose federal common law suits, the
case eliminated an important potential legal source of claims for
addressing the harms of greenhouse gases.

Juliana v. United States (pending in the 9th Circuit Court of Appeals)—
A climate justice suit, filed in 2015, which was brought by twenty-
one young people. It claims that young people have a constitutional right to be protected from climate change (and, more
particularly, that climate change risks deprive young people of
their "rights to life, liberty, property, and public trust resources
by federal government acts that knowingly destroy, endanger, and
impair the unalienable climate system that nature endows"). The
decision could have important implications for attempts to use the
U.S. court system to address climate change risk.

Council on Environmental Quality required agencies to address climate change impacts in their NEPA analyses; although this guidance was withdrawn in 2017, many agencies continue to analyze climate impacts in their NEPA analyses.

Courts' Role in Climate Change Law and Policy

Courts continue to play an important role in U.S. climate law and policy, primarily by acting as a backstop on executive control of agencies in this area, in which Presidents are otherwise largely unchecked. Importantly, the Supreme Court has held that the CAA precludes federal common law on climate change, significantly curtailing the relevance of common law to climate change and further establishing U.S. federal courts as players in climate policy primarily through their role in statutory interpretation and regulatory review, rather than their role as arbiters of the common law (see spotlight 22).

TAKEAWAYS

✓ Although the United States is a party to the United Nations Framework Convention on Climate Change, the United States is not a party to any major international mitigation agreement and has no overarching legislative strategy for addressing mitigation.

✓ U.S. policy is driven by the President, who directs administrative agencies, and by courts, which review agency actions. As a result, U.S. climate policy is particularly political and subject to change with presidential elections.

✓ The Clean Air Act, first drafted in 1970, does not explicitly address greenhouse gases or climate change. It does, however, require the Environmental Protection Agency to regulate any substance that it finds "causes, or contributes to, air pollution which may reasonably be anticipated to endanger public health or welfare." Courts have held that this means that the EPA must regulate any GHGs that justify such an endangerment finding.

DISCUSSION QUESTIONS

1. Should countries set their mitigation policies by reference to the harm their emissions cause to the whole world, or just within their own borders? Why might it be tempting to adopt the domestic-only strategy?

2. Are there tools countries might use to encourage other countries to address global impacts?

3. The United States lacks a modern legislative approach to climate change; the statute with the greatest impact on climate policy, the Clean Air Act, was first drafted in 1970, before climate change was widely recognized as an anthropogenic phenomenon. How might attempting to shoehorn that law into managing climate change create difficulties, given the peculiar challenges associated with regulating climate change to begin with?

4. Do you think courts should play a bigger role in the mitigation of climate change? Or do you think their role should be focused on the effects of climate change?

5. How should policymakers decide what is the right level of mitigation efforts? What kind of information should they use?

ADAPTATION AND NATURAL HAZARDS
DEFINITION

Climate change adaptation involves adjusting to expected or experienced changes to reduce the damage they cause. Adaptation includes the management of natural hazards, or risks from natural phenomena, that may have negative effects on humans or the environment.

DISTINCTIVE CHALLENGES OF ADAPTATION POLICY
AND MANAGING NATURAL HAZARDS

One important and fundamental challenge in adaptation policy is determining the extent to which it makes sense to invest in adapting to the impacts of climate change, versus attempting to mitigate the impacts of climate change before they happen. In some cases, where resources are scarce, this requires a trade-off between investment in mitigation and adaptation strategies.

Regardless of any mitigating measures that are undertaken, however, some degree of climatic change has already happened, and there is little doubt that significantly more will occur over the coming decades. These changes will be disruptive to human life. The extent of this disruption will depend on the scale of the changes that take place and the measures that have been taken to prepare for—and adapt to—these impacts.

There are several distinct challenges to creating successful adaptation policy to address climate change. First, the temporal and geographic diffusion of the effects of climate change poses challenges both for international climate law and for national and regional policymakers. Given the long time horizons involved and the geographic differences of likely impacts (even within countries), choices about the appropriate level of preparation for effects of climate change are likely to be domestically as well as internationally fraught. Consider, for example, that the southeastern United States is expected to be significantly more affected by climate change than other regions of the country. Many of the risks faced in the Southeast—including coastal loss and hurricane risk—are not faced by other U.S. regions, and other risks—including that of deadly heat waves—are much exacerbated by the Southeast's existing warm climate. The Southeast also happens to be relatively poorer than most other U.S. regions, which complicates adaptation efforts further, because the region may require financing from the federal government and, indirectly, from other states. This dynamic also takes place at the international level, with the global South being disproportionately affected by climate change and with pressure being placed on the North to support adaptation through climate financing.

A second, related challenge is the complexity of the effects of climate change and the moving target this represents for adaptation efforts. Changes in weather patterns—such as rising temperatures or more or less precipitation—are problematic both "directly," in terms of heat waves, droughts, or floods, and "indirectly," through ecosystem degradation. Such degradation can result in the extinction (or flourishing!) of particular animal and plant species. This may be important in its own right, and can also be dangerous to human health and welfare. For example, climate change increases the number and geographic range of disease-carrying ticks, including those that cause Lyme disease, and of mosquitoes in the genus *Aedes,* which spread the Zika, chikungunya, dengue fever, and West Nile viruses.

Third, the nonhuman impacts of climate change—for instance, the irreversible damage to ecosystems and/or species—are hard to quantify without human "side effects" (such as the one just mentioned). This makes the trade-off between costly adaptation investments even more difficult, given the great uncertainty about future effects.

Finally, climate change is causing a series of impacts that humans have not seen before, or at least not in recent human history. Many of these impacts are extreme and catastrophic. Natural hazards present an important example of high-magnitude impacts of climate change: climate change is increasing the frequency and magnitude of risks from natural phenomena that may have negative effects on humans or the environment, including floods, wildfire, and hurricanes.

Managing the risks of natural hazards highlights the tension between adaptation and mitigation policy: determining the extent to which it makes sense to invest in adapting to the impacts of climate change— versus attempting to mitigate the impacts of climate change before they happen—is extremely challenging. The likelihood and impact of natural hazards can be greatly reduced through mitigation. Policymakers can therefore also choose to invest in adaptive strategies to make such hazards less damaging when they arise. When resources—or political will—are scarce, policymakers may have to choose between mitigation and adaptation.

KEY U.S. APPROACHES TO CLIMATE CHANGE ADAPTATION AND NATURAL HAZARDS

Adaptation

There is no federal legislative adaptation plan for the United States. Adaptation played an important part in President Obama's climate policies, and he issued a number of executive orders directed toward promoting adaptation planning. During his presidency, over thirty federal agencies adopted climate change adaptation plans tailored to their individual statutory mandates. Because these plans were adopted pursuant to presidential rather than congressional authority, however, they are subject to change under subsequent Presidents. And indeed, President Trump has rescinded the majority of President Obama's executive orders on climate change. Absent congressional action on climate adaptation, subsequent Presidents presumably have similar authority to rescind President Trump's orders. In the meantime, the status of agencies' Obama-era climate adaptation plans remains somewhat ambiguous.[22]

While the status of federal adaptation plans is somewhat unclear, the EPA also runs supportive programs for a number of subnational actors, with the goal of providing research and informational support on a number of adaptive programs. This has included working with state, local, and tribal stakeholders on water resources, particularly through the EPA's Climate Ready Water Utilities and Climate Ready Estuaries programs; providing technical assistance, analytical tools, and outreach support for subnational actors on adaptation through its State and Local Climate and Energy Program; and implementing its own statutes—such as Superfund—to require planning for future climate change.

Natural Hazard Policy

In the United States, federal disaster preparedness and response is administered primarily through the Federal Emergency Management Agency (FEMA). The Robert T. Stafford Disaster Relief and Emergency Assistance Act of 1988 is the primary federal natural hazards legislation; it gives FEMA the responsibility to coordinate government-wide relief efforts, and encourages states and localities to develop their own disaster preparedness plans. The statute does not identify or address the particular relationship between climate change and natural hazards, and FEMA has been increasingly criticized for its handling of climate-related disasters, including Hurricane Katrina in 2004 and Hurricanes Harvey, Irma, and Maria in 2017.

The United States currently experiences approximately $100 billion a year in damage from extreme weather and natural hazards. Floods, the most common of these and the most damaging, will likely continue to increase in severity and magnitude with sea-level rise and precipitation changes. The U.S. Congress has taken steps to update the National Flood Insurance Program, which was first established in 1968, to ensure that FEMA uses "the best available science regarding future changes in sea levels, precipitation, and intensity of hurricanes" to calculate future flood risks.

TAKEAWAYS

✓ The United States has no overarching national mitigation strategy. Congress has not adopted any such strategy, and presidential policies on adaptation are subject to rescission by subsequent Presidents.

✓ Disaster preparedness and response is primarily administered by the Federal Emergency Management Agency. Floods are the most common and damaging disaster in the United States and are projected to increase in severity and magnitude with sea-level rise and precipitation changes. The United States administers a national Flood Insurance Program to underwrite flood risk.

DISCUSSION QUESTIONS

1. How much should countries focus on adaptation rather than mitigation? Which is worse: a country that lacks a cohesive mitigation plan or a country that lacks a cohesive adaptation plan? Must planning for either phenomenon be centralized or might substantial headway be made even with decentralized or ad hoc policies?

2. Should mitigation strategies focus on catastrophes and disasters, like floods and hurricanes, or on pervasive but smaller changes, such as climate shifts that undermine aquatic ecosystems? If a country cares about both kinds of impacts—catastrophic and chronic—does it make sense to plan for both at the same time, or are different strategies needed to manage them?

SUBNATIONAL APPROACHES
DEFINITION

Subnational approaches to climate change include laws and policies adopted by state, county, and city governments.

DISTINCTIVE ASPECTS OF SUBNATIONAL CLIMATE APPROACHES

Understanding subnational approaches to climate change in the United States can be complicated because the diversity of actors creates significant variance in strategies, and because the interplay between multiple actors can generate complexities of its own. In some cases, larger subnational entities, such as states, can have different strategies and interests than other subnational entities, such as cities. And different subnational actors—such as coastal southern states and landlocked agricultural states—may have different strategies and interests as well. Still, a few dynamics of subnational climate actors arise relatively frequently and are worth noting.

First, even more so than with domestic climate policy, subnational climate policies face a special challenge in addressing the coordination problems generated by climate-changing emissions. Basically, any subnational actor that invests in reducing its GHG emissions is unlikely to reap all—if any—of the impacts of those emissions reductions, even as it bears most (or all) of the cost. Other cities, states, nation-states, and regions are likely to receive a free ride on those emissions reductions and, absent some form of coordination, may have little or no incentive to adopt reciprocal emissions reductions. In some cases, as where cities or states are competing with one another to attract industry, this can create competitive disadvantages for subnational entities that adopt policies penalizing emissions.

One strategy for addressing the problem of externalized benefits is for subnational entities to invest in adaptation strategies (whose impacts are generally more local) rather than mitigation strategies (whose impacts are generally global). While this strategy can help prevent externalization of benefits, adaptation investments can generate puzzles of their own. First, it can sometimes be politically challenging to generate revenue for large adaptation projects for risks that may not materialize for many years to come. Second, selecting appropriate adaptation projects requires management of complex and uncertain science—not only about the likely local impacts of climate change, the models for which remain uncertain, but also about the likely impact of selected adaptation strategies on those impacts. This creates a significant informational burden for subnational governments.

Another common strategy for subnational entities is to pursue climate strategies that generate local co-benefits—for example, by banning diesel-powered buses that generate both GHG emissions and local air pollutants. This approach can help address the political challenge of eliciting investment in climate projects, and in some cases—as where the co-benefits of the climate actions are relatively well understood—it can also help with the informational burden of managing local climate-impact predictions.

The informational burdens of climate change fall particularly hard on subnational entities, which typically have fewer resources for researching and developing expertise on climate change issues. As a result, subnational entities must often rely on research generated outside their borders—either at the national level, in other countries, or through general scientific research. This can prove particularly problematic where the subnational entity is particularly interested in local climate impacts.

KEY SUBNATIONAL APPROACHES TO CLIMATE CHANGE

The lack of significant international climate commitments, and of national climate legislation, has opened significant opportunity for subnational actors in the United States—particularly states and cities—to develop their own approaches to climate change mitigation and adaptation.

Important State Approaches

U.S. states have adopted varying approaches to climate change. For most states, climate change policy is administered through the state's environmental agency. But some states have done more. Notably, in 2017, several states announced the establishment of the U.S. Climate Alliance, a coalition of Governors committed to reducing GHG emissions consistent with the goals of the Paris Agreement. The alliance includes more than fifteen states and over 40 percent of the U.S. population. Another state coalition of nine eastern states administers

SPOTLIGHT 23. CALIFORNIA

California has adopted an extensive body of climate change law and policy at the state level. California, which would be the fifth largest economy in the world if it were a separate nation, accounts for a bit less than 1 percent of global greenhouse gas emissions (and about 7 percent of U.S. emissions). Its average annual per capita emissions is 9.26 tons, compared to the national average of 16.5 tons per capita.

California has taken an aggressive approach to climate change since at least 2007, when its Global Warming Solutions Act capped carbon dioxide emissions. It has set a stringent goal—to reduce its emissions to 40 percent below 1990 levels by 2030—through a series of strategies: by increasing renewable electricity production to 50 percent; reducing petroleum use in vehicles by 50 percent; doubling energy efficiency savings at existing buildings; reducing greenhouse gas emissions from land use; and reducing short-lived climate pollutants. It continues to operate a carbon cap-and-trade program through its Air Resources Board, and administers a wide portfolio of state-level incentives for promoting high-efficiency automobiles and electricity use.

the Regional Greenhouse Gas Initiative, which has cut electricity-related GHG emissions almost in half since 2009. Other states do little or nothing to address climate change. Several Governors, such as Chris Sununu in New Hampshire and Rick Scott in Florida, are skeptical of climate change science. Many other states—particularly those that rely heavily on resource extraction—have no state policies. Most states still lack a state climate adaptation plan. Currently, the state with the most extensive body of climate law and policy is California (see spotlight 23).

Important City Approaches

U.S. cities, even more than states, have a widely varying approach to climate change policy. In the wake of the national U.S. withdrawal from the Paris Agreement, however, many of the largest cities in the country—including New York, Chicago, and Atlanta—have set emissions reduction goals of 80 percent or higher by 2050, aligning with the goals of the Paris Agreement. Cities are not empowered to join treaties under U.S. law, but of course such commitments may still be made and kept. Many other cities have adopted targeted adaptation strategies to adjust for expected local climate impacts. New York City's adaptation plan is particularly ambitious (see spotlight 24).

SPOTLIGHT 24. NEW YORK CITY

New York City has one of the world's most ambitious urban climate adaptation plans, launched in 2013 in response to the $19 billion in damage caused by Superstorm Sandy. At a cost of $19.5 billion, it details 250 climate adaptation strategies that will attempt to prepare the city for rising seas, increased weather and hurricane risk, and an increase in dangerous heat waves. New York has hired its own panel of climate change scientists, drawn from some of the country's best research universities, and created its own hyperlocal climate models for predicting local climate impacts.

TAKEAWAYS

✓ In the absence of any comprehensive international or federal strategy for addressing climate change, subnational actors in the United States have the opportunity to play an outsized role in addressing climate change.

✓ Views of the practical and moral impact of climate change vary substantially across the United States. As a result, many states and cities are often faced with a situation where they disagree strongly with national U.S. climate policy. In response, cities and states have widely diverging subnational climate policies.

✓ Some states, perhaps most notably California, have adopted statewide policies that attempt to aggressively address climate mitigation and adaptation.

✓ In the wake of the U.S. withdrawal from the Paris Agreement, many of the largest cities in the country have aligned their goals with those of the agreement.

DISCUSSION QUESTIONS

1. The causes of climate change are global, but many of the impacts are local. What does this suggest may be the best use of subnational actors in addressing climate change? Should their participation be focused on mitigation, adaptation, both, or neither?

2. Subnational climate policies vary substantially across the United States. As a result, even nearby cities may have very different incentives for development and growth. What difficulties might arise from this fragmentation of climate policies?

CLIMATE CHANGE: SUMMARY

The United States is a significant contributor to both historical and current greenhouse gas emissions. While it is a member of the UN Framework Convention on Climate Change, the United States has refused to ratify any international agreements that would bind it to reduce its GHG emissions. The United States also has no comprehensive legislative policy regarding climate change mitigation or adaptation. Nevertheless, U.S. domestic policy has resulted in at least a 12 percent decrease in emissions since 2005.

In the absence of international obligations and congressional direction, U.S. climate policy is substantially influenced by presidential policy, as implemented through administrative agencies. As a result, U.S. climate change policy can change substantially with presidential administrations. This has left room for subnational actors, including states and cities, to play an increasing role in generating commitments to reduce emissions and in implementing adaptation strategies.

KEY TERMS

ADAPTATION Adjusting to expected or experienced changes.

CLIMATE CHANGE Changes in global climate patterns, specifically those occurring since the late twentieth century, that are attributable largely to increased levels of atmospheric carbon dioxide produced by the use of fossil fuels.

COLLECTIVE ACTION PROBLEM A situation in which people are disincentivized to pursue a joint or common goal.

ENERGY EFFICIENCY The process of reducing energy consumption by using less energy to achieve the same amount of useful output.

FREE-RIDER PROBLEM A situation that occurs when those who benefit from resources, public goods, or other actions do not pay for them, resulting in the underprovision of such goods or actions.

GREENHOUSE GAS A gas that contributes to the greenhouse effect.

MITIGATION Attempts to limit the magnitude and rate of long-term climate change, primarily through reducing anthropogenic greenhouse gas emissions.

NATURAL HAZARDS Naturally occurring physical phenomena caused either by rapid- or slow-onset events, such as earthquakes, avalanches, droughts, or floods.

SOCIAL COST OF CARBON A monetized estimate of the expected impact (either globally or domestically) of emitting a set quantity of carbon dioxide.

DISCUSSION QUESTIONS

1. Should the United States focus more on mitigation or adaptation in the coming decades? Which do you think will be more important globally? Locally?

2. In the absence of ratified international obligations or comprehensive climate legislation, U.S. climate policy is subject to substantial changes with different presidential administrations. What challenges do you foresee this posing to creating effective climate law and policy? Are those challenges worse for mitigation or adaptation? Are there benefits to the United States to having climate policy change substantially with the election of each new President?

NOTES

1. There is a small but persistent group of politicians and scholars that question the existence of climate change or its anthropogenic causes. While the existence of this group raises interesting questions, we will focus on the mainstream scientific consensus that is reflected in the reports of the Intergovernmental Panel on Climate Change, available at www.ipcc.ch/publications_and_data/publications_and_data_reports.shtml.

2. See, e.g., Horst Rittel and Melvin Webber, *Dilemmas in a General Theory of Planning*, 4 POL. SCI. 155 (1973), for an early definition of wicked problems and their characteristics.

3. By some measures, global temperature increase by 2100 will be approximately 24 percent attributable to past and present emissions by the United States. See Climate Analytics, HISTORICAL RESPONSIBILITY FOR CLIMATE CHANGE—FROM COUNTRIES [*sic*] EMISSIONS TO CONTRIBUTION TO TEMPERATURE INCREASE (Nov. 2015), http://climateanalytics.org/files/historical_responsibility_report_nov_2015.pdf.

4. See International Energy Agency, CO_2 EMISSIONS FROM FUEL COMBUSTION (2017), retrieved from www.iea.org/.

5. Low-emission countries, by contrast, vary significantly in how they achieve low emissions: the lowest per capita emissions are in Denmark (0.06) and Finland (0.09), wealthy and highly developed nations that have invested heavily in emissions abatement. Other low per capita emitters, such as South Sudan (0.13), Myanmar (0.14), and Tanzania (0.2), have low emissions because they lack industries that generate substantial emissions.

6. See World Resources Institute, *The Top 10 Emitting States Contribute Half of U.S. Emissions,* www.wri.org/blog/2017/08/6-charts-understand-us-state-greenhouse-gas-emissions (listing Texas, California, Pennsylvania, Illinois, Ohio, Florida, Indiana, Louisiana, New York, and Michigan as the top ten U.S. emitters).

7. As of 2017, the majority of energy in the United States (62 percent, or 2,516 billion kWh/4,015 billion kWh) is generated by fossil fuels. Of these, natural gas provides the greatest share (31.7 percent), with coal (30.1 percent) close behind and with petroleum providing only a minimal share (0.5 percent). See U.S. Energy Information Administration, www.eia.gov/tools/faqs/faq.php?id = 427&t = 3.

8. See World Resources Institute, *The U.S. Energy Sector Contributes 84 Percent of the Country's Total Emissions,* www.wri.org/blog/2017/08/6-charts-understand-us-state-greenhouse-gas-emissions.

9. See U.S. Global Change Research Program, www.globalchange.gov /browse. For a quick summary of climate change impacts within the United States, building on the National Climate Assessment, see National Aeronautics and Space Administration, *Effects: How Climate Is Changing,* https://climate.nasa.gov/effects/.

10. This 2014 study by the Yale Project on Climate Change Communication found that 63 percent of Americans believed global warming is happening, though only 48 percent believed that climate change is mostly caused by human activities, with 35 percent ascribing it to natural changes. The study's results are conveniently summarized online at http://environment.yale.edu/poe/v2014/.

11. See Seth Motel, *Polls Show Most Americans Believe in Climate Change, but Give It Low Priority,* Pew Research Center, Sept. 23, 2014, www.pewresearch.org/fact-tank/2014/09/23/most-americans-believe-in-climate-change-but-

give-it-low-priority/ (e.g., in 2010, 9 percent of Americans reported climate change as the most important problem for the United States as a whole).

12. See the Yale Project on Climate Change Communication, *supra* note 10 (finding that 79 percent of Americans who do not believe climate change is happening identify as Republican or Republican-leaning, compared to 32 percent of all Americans; and that 68 percent identify as politically conservative, compared to 30 percent of all Americans).

13. Tien Ming Lee et al., *Predictors of Public Climate Change Awareness and Risk Perception Around the World*, 5 NATURE CLIMATE CHANGE 1014 (Nov. 2015).

14. UNFCCC, Article 2.

15. Paris Agreement, Article 4.

16. See generally Conference of the Parties, UNITED NATIONS FRAMEWORK CONVENTION ON CLIMATE CHANGE, COPENHAGEN, DEN., DEC. 7–19, 2009, REPORT OF THE CONFERENCE OF THE PARTIES ON ITS FIFTEENTH SESSION, U.N. Doc. FCCC/CP/2009/11/Add.1 (Mar. 30, 2010).

17. See www.epa.gov/ghgreporting for detailed information about greenhouse gas emissions. The data can be filtered in a variety of ways, including by facility, industry, location, and gas.

18. See *id.*, claiming that "America must help forge a truly global solution to this global challenge by galvanizing international action to significantly reduce emissions (particularly among the major emitting countries), prepare for climate impacts, and drive progress through the international negotiations."

19. See note 17.

20. NOAA maintains a series of climate resources at www.noaa.gov /climate. The National Centers for Environmental Information is accessible at www.ncei.noaa.gov/.

21. For more on the use and calculation of the social cost of carbon, see William Pizer et al., *Using and Improving the Social Cost of Carbon*, 346 SCIENCE 1189 (2014).

22. For some of the complexities here, see Kevin Todd, *Climate Change Adaptation Plans: What Will Be the Impact of President Trump's Rescission of Obama Era Policies?*, MICH. J. ENVTL. & ADMIN. L. (2018).

Conclusions

Over the relatively short period of our existence, we humans have changed the Earth's environment in profound ways—and we will continue to do so. But with understanding and care, we can choose to act with knowledge about the likely impacts of our behaviors and to regulate those behaviors through law and by other means. This book aims to create a starting point for more and deeper conversation between those working in environmental sciences (in the broadest sense), foreign jurisdictions, and U.S. lawyers in order to create the best possible answers to complicated social and environmental questions of how humans should shape their environments.

One of the main goals of this book was to present distinctive features of the U.S. approach to environmental law. As you will have seen in the collection of legal snapshots in part two, the actual legal instruments applied to different environmental impacts are varied and numerous. Despite their many differences, they also reflect defining features of the U.S. legal system: federalism, the role of administrative agencies, and the centrality of risk analysis and cost-benefit analysis. Learning to identify common strands can help in making sense of seemingly dissimilar, or even conflicting, U.S. approaches to different environmental problems, as well as provide a basis for comparison between U.S. approaches and those adopted by other countries.

In writing this book, we aimed to provide information in such a way that readers can make their own independent assessments of the U.S. approach to environmental law. However, this is not to say that the law is normatively neutral. The status quo of U.S. environmental law should not be taken as a natural phenomenon, but as the result of human decision making. This means that moving forward, humans have the opportunity to change and to improve legal rules, in the United States and around the world.

Acknowledgments

These books are the result of a lengthy process that started in 2015. During this time, many people have contributed to their eventual shape and form. These acknowledgments do not attempt to be comprehensive in their mention of these people. We are grateful to work in a part of academia that is characterized by so many supportive, creative, and generous colleagues.

For the U.S. volume, we would specifically like to thank Blake Bacon, Stephanie Davidson, Richard Earles, Alfred Heikamp, Molly Lindsey, John Nagle, Jonathan Nash, Petra Siebelink, and Edwin Woerdman, as well as members of the Society for Environmental Law and Economics, our students, and our families for their contributions to making this a better book. We would also like to thank UC Press for their confidence in the project.

Finally, we would like to thank one another for a delightful coauthorship.

Time Line of U.S. Environmental Law

Declaration of
Independence from
Great Britain
1776

First Congress
convened under a ratified
U.S. Constitution
1789

Forest Reserve Act of
1891 creates the National
Forest System
1891

Passage of Atomic
Energy Act, promoting
use of atomic energy
1954

National Wildlife
Refuge System
established
1940

National Park
System established
1916

Rachel Carson's book *Silent Spring* is
published, jump-starting the environmental
movement and highlighting the environmental
impacts of toxic substances
1962

The Cuyahoga River in Ohio
is so polluted that it catches on fire,
bringing national attention to
water pollution issues
1969

Creation of the
Environmental
Protection Agency
1970

Passage of the
Clean Air Act
1970

Passage of the
National Environmental
Policy Act
1970

Celebration of the first
"Earth Day," on April
22, 1970
1970

EPA bans the pesticide DDT, a cheap and
effective pesticide, because of its significant
impacts on wildlife and the environment
1972

EPA begins phasing
out lead in gasoline
1973

Passage of the
Endangered Species
Act
1973

Passage of the
Clean Water Act
1972

National oil embargo triggers a
spike in oil prices, stimulating
conservation and research into
alternative energy
1973

Passage of the
Safe Drinking
Water Act
1974

Passage of the
Resource Conservation
and Recovery Act
1976

Amendment of the
Clean Water Act
1977

Amendment of the
Clean Air Act
1977

Passage of the
Toxic Substances
Control Act
1976

Love Canal disaster discovered: a small town
in New York is found to be contaminated by
buried, leaking chemical containers, linked to
serious health threats
1978

A severe meltdown of the Three Mile
Island nuclear power plant provokes
controversy about nuclear power safety
1979

Passage of the Comprehensive
Environmental Response, Compensation,
and Liability Act ("Superfund")
1980

Executive Order 12,291, the first executive
order requiring agencies to do cost-benefit
analysis, is signed by President Ronald Reagan
1981

Amendment of
the Safe Drinking
Water Act
1986

Amendment of the Resource Conservation and
Recovery Act to include Hazardous and Solid
Waste Amendments
1984

Passage of the
Nuclear Waste
Policy Act
1982

Passage of the Emergency
Planning and Community
Right-to-Know Act
1986

United States signs the
Montreal Protocol to
protect the ozone layer
1987

Congress designates Yucca
Mountain, Nevada, as the sole
repository site for nuclear waste
1987

Exxon Valdez spills 11 million
gallons of crude oil into Alaska's
Prince William Sound
1989

Passage of the Marine Protection,
Research, and Sanctuaries Act (also
known as the "Ocean Dumping Act")
1988

Amendment of the Clean Air
Act, including creation of a
sulfur dioxide trading scheme
to address acid rain
1990

Passage of
the Pollution
Prevention Act
1990

Release of the Flavr Savr
tomato, the first genetically
modified food approved for release
in the United States by Calgene
1994

Department of Energy
terminates efforts to license
a nuclear waste repository at
Yucca Mountain
2009

Executive Order 13175 requires
consultation and coordination
with Indian tribal governments,
signed by President Bill Clinton
2000

Amendment of
the Safe Drinking
Water Act
1996

President Barack
Obama announces a
Climate Action Plan
2013

EPA announces a Clean Power Plan
to limit carbon dioxide emissions
from existing power plants
2015

President Obama signs
on to the Paris Agreement
on Climate Change
2016

EPA rescinds the Clean Power
Plan and replaces it with the
Affordable Clean Energy Rule
2019

President Donald Trump announces
intent to withdraw from the Paris
Agreement on Climate Change
2017

Additional Resources

The purpose of this book is to present an accessible introduction to, and overview of, the environmental law of the United States. In many cases, readers may now wish to know more about particular environmental laws, or to research primary source material. This section is intended to point readers toward helpful additional resources for further study.

ACCESSING U.S. ENVIRONMENTAL LAWS

Throughout the book, we have referred to a number of different sources of law, including the U.S. Constitution, statutes, regulations, and judicial decisions.

For access to the U.S. Constitution, the U.S. Code (in which federal statutes are published), the Code of Federal Regulations (in which federal regulations are published), and Supreme Court cases, the Legal Information Institute maintains free online resources at www.law.cornell.edu/.

The Environmental Protection Agency (EPA) maintains significant information about environmental problems in the United States, as well as the actions it is taking to protect the environment, at www.epa.gov. The EPA publishes filings, procedures, and orders for its administrative law judges at www.epa.gov/alj.

Two particularly useful online research guides, which maintain links to a number of further resources, are the Vermont Law School's Resource Directory at http://forms.vermontlaw.edu/library/resource-directory/ and the UCLA Environmental Law Research Guide at https://libguides.law.ucla.edu /environmental.

FURTHER READING ON U.S. LAW

For more in-depth information on the U.S. legal system, we recommend two books:

> E. Allan Farnsworth, *An Introduction to the Legal System of the United States* (4th ed., Oxford University Press, 2010), an accessible overview of the modern U.S. legal system
>
> Lawrence M. Friedman, *A History of American Law* (4th ed., Oxford University Press, 2019), a classic that provides a rich historical account of the development of U.S. law

FURTHER READING ON U.S. ENVIRONMENTAL LAW

For a readable, in-depth discussion of the history and development of U.S. environmental law, written by one of the leading U.S. scholars in environmental law, we recommend Richard Lazarus, *The Making of Environmental Law* (University of Chicago Press, 2006). Readers looking for more traditional secondary summaries of U.S. environmental law, directed toward U.S. law students, have a number of good options:

> For pollution control, two we particularly like—both by well-regarded U.S. legal scholars—are Jonathan R. Nash, *Environmental Law and Policy: Essentials* (Aspen, 2010), and Daniel Farber, *Environmental Law in a Nutshell* (10th ed., West Academic, 2019).
>
> For a treatment of natural resources and their relationship with ecosystem management, we recommend Josh Eagle et al., *Natural Resources Law and Policy: Concepts and Insights* (Foundation Press, 2017).
>
> For further treatment of climate change law and policy, we highly recommend Dan Farber and Cinnamon Carlarne, *Climate Change Law: Concepts and Insights* (Foundation Press, 2017).
>
> The most commonly used environmental law textbook in U.S. law school courses is Robert V. Percival et al., *Environmental Regulation: Law, Science, and Policy* (8th ed., Wolters Kluwer, 2018). It includes a particularly robust treatment of U.S. pollution control law, as well as briefer sections on natural resources and climate change.

STATE AND LOCAL ENVIRONMENTAL LAW

This book is focused on federal U.S. environmental law. In many cases, however, state and local laws also play a critical role in shaping the U.S. environment.

A classic resource for state environmental laws is Daniel Selmi and Kenneth Manaster's annually updated treatise *State Environmental Law;* it has particularly detailed treatment of state air and water quality control, hazardous waste management, and the cleanup of contaminated sites. Unfortunately, it is available only behind a paywall (online at WestlawNext).

The Environmental Protection Agency maintains an updated list of state environmental agencies, which in turn provide links to state and local legal resources, at www.epa.gov/home/health-and-environmental-agencies-us-states-and-territories.

For online access to state and local environmental statutes, we recommend the free resources provided by the Legal Information Institute. They maintain a particularly good listing of state statutes regarding natural resources at www.law.cornell.edu/wex/table_natural_resources.

COMPARATIVE RESOURCES

For readers interested in comparative environmental law, we recommend the following:

Josephine van Zeben and Arden Rowell, *A Guide to EU Environmental Law* (University of California Press, 2020), the companion to this volume, designed to allow for easy comparison between the environmental laws of the United States and the European Union

Emma Lees and Jorge E. Viñuales (editors), *The Oxford Handbook of Comparative Environmental Law* (Oxford University Press, 2019), a recent resource on comparative environmental law, directed toward comparative legal scholars

PANDEMIC-ERA RESOURCES

The COVID-19 pandemic may have important impacts on the future of environmental law.

For a discussion of the types of legal change triggered by the pandemic, see Arden Rowell, "COVID-19 and Environmental Law," *50 Environmental Law Reporter* 10881 (2020).

For updates on how the U.S. Environmental Protection Agency is responding to the pandemic, see www.epa.gov/coronavirus.

Glossary

ACTS Laws created by a federal or state legislature (aka *statutes*).

ADAPTATION Adjusting to expected or experienced changes.

ADMINISTRATIVE LAW Law that governs administrative agencies.

ADMINISTRATIVE PROCEDURE Rules that govern procedures used by agencies and in agency proceedings.

AGENCIES Units of government created by statute.

AIR POLLUTION Higher-than-normal concentrations of materials, including chemicals, that are out of place in air.

BEHAVIORAL INSTRUMENTS Instruments for regulating behavior that build on social science research, particularly in psychology and behavioral economics.

BILLS Legislative proposals that have not yet been voted on by the legislature.

BIODIVERSITY The variety of life in a habitat or ecosystem.

CAP-AND-TRADE SYSTEM A regulatory instrument that sets a maximum cap on a certain activity (e.g., emitting activities) and allows participants to trade permits with each other to engage in more or less of that activity.

CHECKS AND BALANCES A model of governance that limits the concentration of power by giving each of the branches of government the authority to limit the power of the other(s).

CHOICE ARCHITECTURE Purposeful structuring of decision-making contexts to shape people's behavior toward selected ends.

CITIZEN SUIT A lawsuit brought by a private citizen to enforce the law.

CIVIL LAW A legal system that codifies core principles into referable systems, such as statutes.

CIVIL PROCEDURE The rules that must be followed in noncriminal judicial courts.

CLIMATE CHANGE Changes in global climate patterns, specifically those occurring since the late twentieth century, that are attributable largely to increased levels of atmospheric carbon dioxide produced by the use of fossil fuels.

COLLECTIVE ACTION PROBLEM A situation in which people are disincentivized to pursue a joint or common goal.

COMMAND-AND-CONTROL REGULATION A group of regulatory instruments that rely on standard setting in order to permit or ban certain types of behavior.

COMMERCE CLAUSE Clause of the U.S. Constitution that allows the federal government to regulate issues that (may) affect foreign or interstate trade.

COMMON LAW Law made by judges, published in the form of judicial opinions, which gives precedential authority to prior court decisions (may be public or private law).

COMPENSATORY MITIGATION Allowing for the degradation of one habitat, such as a wetland, in exchange for improving (or even creating) a different habitat.

COMPLEX IMPACTS Environmental impacts that are obscure, technical, and/or interactive. These can be difficult to measure, understand, and regulate.

COMPLIANCE COSTS The cost of complying with a regulatory standard.

CONSERVATION The protection of a natural environment or species.

CONSTITUTIONAL LAW Law that provides for the structure and functioning of a government—for how the government is "constituted"—and how the government is supposed to interact with individuals (a form of public law).

CONTRACT LAW Law that governs how promises between individuals are enforced (a form of private law).

COOPERATIVE FEDERALISM System of cooperation between federal and state governments, commonly used in the implementation of U.S. pollution control statutes.

COST-BENEFIT ANALYSIS A decision procedure for quantifying (and typically monetizing) the expected positive and negative impacts of a proposed policy.

CRIMINAL LAW Law that governs the punishment and behavior of those who commit crimes—behaviors that are considered so socially damaging that they are punishable by law (a form of public law).

CRIMINAL PROCEDURE Rules that govern criminal legal procedures.

CRITERIA POLLUTANTS Common air pollutants for which the Environmental Protection Agency sets National Ambient Air Quality Standards under the Clean Air Act.

DEFAULT RULES A preset course of action that takes effect automatically, unless decision makers provide an alternative specification.

DIFFUSE IMPACTS Environmental impacts that are geographically and/or spatially distant from the human actions that caused them.

DISCOUNTING The process of making future (monetary) amounts comparable to current amounts.

DOSE-RESPONSE Relationship between the amount of a substance an organism is exposed to and the harm and response the exposure causes.

ECONOMIC INSTRUMENTS Regulatory instruments that rely on economic incentives in order to achieve compliance.

ECOSYSTEMS Geographic areas where living entities (plants, animals, and other organisms) and nonliving entities (water, air, and soil) interact in mutually interdependent ways.

ENERGY EFFICIENCY The process of reducing energy consumption by using less energy to achieve the same amount of useful output.

ENVIRONMENT The surroundings or conditions in which humans, plants, and animals function.

ENVIRONMENTAL IMPACTS Consequences (generally of human actions) for the surroundings or conditions in which humans, plants, and animals function.

ENVIRONMENTAL JUSTICE Fair distribution of environmental impacts.

ENVIRONMENTAL LAW The use of law to regulate human behaviors with environmental impacts.

EXECUTIVE ORDERS Legal directives created by the President to execute law.

EXPOSURE REDUCTION Amending behavior so that there is less exposure to pollution and, thus (hopefully) less harm.

EXTERNALITIES Costs or benefits created by an activity that are experienced by parties other than the one engaged in the activity.

FEDERALISM System (and principle) of government in which several states form a union for some purposes while remaining independent for others.

FRAMING A behavioral instrument that uses small changes in how contextual cues are presented to strategically shape people's behaviors.

FREE-RIDER PROBLEM A situation that occurs when those who benefit from resources, public goods, or other actions do not pay for them, resulting in the underprovision of such goods or actions.

GENETIC MODIFICATION The manipulation of an organism's genes using biotechnology, typically to augment desirable traits or delete undesirable ones.

(GOVERNMENTAL) FUNCTION Responsibilities and powers of government, in the United States, as fulfilled by three branches of government: the legislature, executive, and judiciary.

GREENHOUSE GAS A gas that contributes to the greenhouse effect.

HABITAT The home of an animal, plant, or other organism.

INDIAN The term used in the U.S. Constitution to refer to North American indigenous peoples.

INDIAN COUNTRY All lands in Indian reservations or held in trust for individual Indians or Indian tribes.

INDIAN RESERVATION An area of land reserved for an Indian tribe to live on and use.

INSTRUMENT CHOICE Selection among different types of regulatory instruments with a view to create the "best" fit between the regulated behavior and the method of regulation.

JUDICIAL Of, or relating to, courts or judges.

JURISDICTION The authority to make legally binding decisions within a given territory or subject area.

MARKET-BASED REGULATION A regulation that makes use of economic incentives created by markets.

MITIGATION Attempts to limit the magnitude and rate of long-term climate change, primarily through reducing anthropogenic greenhouse gas emissions.

NATIONAL AMBIENT AIR QUALITY STANDARDS (NAAQS) Health-based standards set under the Clean Air Act for the quantity of criteria pollutants that may be in the air.

NATURAL HAZARDS Naturally occurring physical phenomena caused either by rapid- or slow-onset events, such as earthquakes, avalanches, droughts, or floods.

NONHUMAN IMPACTS Environmental impacts that relate primarily or exclusively to nonhuman animals, plants, and processes.

NONPOINT SOURCE WATER POLLUTION Water pollution that originates from multiple diffuse sources, as from agricultural runoff or drainage through urban streets.

NUDGE A behavioral instrument that is meant to alter people's behavior in predictable ways, without forbidding any options or significantly changing economic incentives.

NUISANCE An act that is unreasonably harmful to the public (public nuisance) or to an individual (private nuisance) and for which there is a judicial remedy.

PATH DEPENDENCY A phenomenon whereby people continue existing practices even where better ones could be adopted, because of the costs associated with shifting to new "paths" or practices.

POINT SOURCE WATER POLLUTION Water pollution that originates from a single identifiable source, such as a pipe or ditch.

POTENTIALLY RESPONSIBLE PARTY (PRP) Under CERCLA, a person or company—including past and current owners—who may be responsible for cleanup costs for a contaminated site.

PREEMPTION A process whereby the law of one level of government displaces the law of another. In the United States, this is most commonly preemption of state law by federal law.

PRIVATE ACTORS Individuals, nongovernmental organizations, or companies acting in their own interest (and not on behalf of the government).

PRIVATE LAW Law that governs relationships between individuals (e.g., contract law, tort law, and property law).

PROPERTY LAW Law about the relationships between people and things.

PUBLIC ACTORS Members of government, or those acting on behalf of the government in an official capacity.

PUBLIC LAW Law that governs issues that affect the general public or state (e.g., constitutional law, administrative law, and criminal law).

RACE TO THE BOTTOM Process whereby (environmental) standards are continually lowered to remain competitive with other jurisdictions.

RATIFICATION Approval of a signed international treaty by Congress.

REGULATIONS Binding rules of legal conduct issued by agencies; may also refer to the action or process, by any legal actor, of limiting or encouraging patterns of behavior.

REGULATORY INSTRUMENT A tool that a policymaker uses to achieve regulatory goals.

RISK ANALYSIS A systemized method for identifying, assessing, quantifying, and evaluating risks.

RISK ASSESSMENT The scientific and technical first "stage" of risk analysis where the probabilities and magnitudes of hazards associated with particular behaviors and policies are identified and quantified.

RISK MANAGEMENT The second "stage" of risk analysis, in which policy-based decisions are made about which and how risks will be reduced or tolerated.

SEPARATION OF POWERS An organizational principle of government whereby the legislative, executive, and judicial functions of the government are assigned to separate actors.

SOCIAL COST OF CARBON A monetized estimate of the expected impact (either globally or domestically) of emitting a set quantity of carbon dioxide.

SOIL POLLUTION Higher-than-normal concentrations of materials, including chemicals, that are out of place in soil.

SOURCE REDUCTION Amending behavior to reduce the amount of pollution initially created (at the "source").

STATUTES Laws created by a federal or state legislature (aka *acts*).

SUSTAINABILITY The use of natural resources in a way that is economically, socially, and environmentally viable in the long term.

TORT A civil (as opposed to criminal) wrong that creates a cause of action for suing in court.

TORT LAW Law that governs how people can use law to receive compensation for harms or injuries that other individuals have caused them (a form of private law).

TOXIC SUBSTANCES Materials, sometimes referred to as "chemicals," that create significant human or nonhuman environmental harm, even when used as intended.

WASTE A material, substance, or byproduct that is discarded as no longer useful.

WATER POLLUTION Higher-than-normal concentrations of materials, including chemicals, that are out of place in water, including drinking water.

WETLANDS Transitional ecosystems that form a link between land and water.

WILDERNESS An area of land that exhibits minimal human impact; in the United States, such lands are protected under the National Wilderness Preservation System.

WILDLIFE Undomesticated animals that live in their natural habitats.

Index

Founded in 1893,
UNIVERSITY OF CALIFORNIA PRESS
publishes bold, progressive books and journals
on topics in the arts, humanities, social sciences,
and natural sciences—with a focus on social
justice issues—that inspire thought and action
among readers worldwide.

The UC PRESS FOUNDATION
raises funds to uphold the press's vital role
as an independent, nonprofit publisher, and
receives philanthropic support from a wide
range of individuals and institutions—and from
committed readers like you. To learn more, visit
ucpress.edu/supportus.

Made in United States
North Haven, CT
31 August 2023

40999521R10164